THE SCOTTISH HISTORIES

SIR
WALTER
SCOTT

GEDDES & GROSSET

This edition published 2001 by Geddes & Grosset,
David Dale House, New Lanark ML11 9DJ, Scotland

© 2001 Geddes & Grosset

Adapted from a text by Professor Saintsbury

ISBN 1 84205 102 4

Printed and bound in Europe

Contents

I Life Till Marriage 9

II Early Literary Work 21

III The Verse Romances 42

IV The Novels, from
Waverley to Redgauntlet 79

V The Downfall of
Ballantyne and Company 120

VI Last Works and Days 137

VII Conclusion 162

Chronology 184

CHAPTER I

*L*IFE TILL MARRIAGE

Scott's own 'autobiographic fragment', printed in
Lockhart's first volume, has made other accounts of his
youth mostly superfluous, even to an age which persists
in knowing better about everything and everybody than
it or they knew about themselves. No one ever recorded
his genealogy more minutely, with greater pride, or with
a more saving sense of humour than Sir Walter. He was
connected, though remotely, with well-born families on
both sides. His great-grandfather was the son of the Laird
of Raeburn, who was grandson of Walter Scott of Harden
and the 'Flower of Yarrow'. The great-grandson, 'Beardie',
acquired that nickname by letting his beard grow like
General Dalziel, though for the exile of James II, instead of the death of Charles I – 'whilk was the waur
reason', as Sir Walter himself might have said.

Beardie's second son, being more thoroughly sickened
of the sea in his first voyage than Robinson Crusoe,
became a farmer and a Whig, and married the daughter
of Haliburton of Newmains – there was also Macdougal

and Campbell blood on the female side of the older generations of the family. Their eldest son Walter, father of Sir Walter, was born in 1729, and, being trained for a legal career, became the original, according to undisputed tradition, of the 'Saunders Fairford' of *Redgauntlet*, the most autobiographical as well as one of the most charming of the novels. He married Anne Rutherford, who, through her mother, brought the blood of the Swintons of Swinton to enrich the joint strain; and from her father, a member of a family distinguished in the annals of the University of Edinburgh, may have transmitted some of the love for books which was not the most prominent feature of the other ingredients.

Walter himself was the third 'permanent child' (to adopt an expression of Mr Traill's about another person) of a family of twelve, only five of whom survived infancy. His three brothers, John, Thomas, and Daniel, and his sister Anne, all figure in the records; but little is heard of John and not much of Anne. Thomas, the second, either had, or was thought by his indulgent brother to have, literary talents, and was at one time put up to father the novels; while Daniel (whose misconduct in money matters, and cowardice, brought on him the only display of anything that can be called rancour recorded in Sir Walter's history) concerns us even less. The date of the novelist's birth was 15 August 1771, the place, 'the top

of the College Wynd', where the Old University build-
ings of Chambers Street are now situated, and near the
site of Kirk of Field. Escaping the real or supposed dan-
gers of a consumptive wet-nurse, he was at first healthy
enough; but around the time of teething he developed
the famous lameness, which at first seemed to threaten
loss of all use of his right leg.

The child was sent to the home of his grandfather,
the Whig farmer of Sandyknowe, where he lived for
some years under the shadow of Smailholm Tower, reading a little, listening to Border legends a great deal, and
making one long journey to London and Bath. This
first blessed period of his childhood lasted until he was
almost eight, and ended with a course of sea-bathing at
Prestonpans, where he met the original in name and
perhaps in nature of Captain Dalgetty, and the original
in character of the *Antiquary*. Then he returned (*circa*
1779) to his father's house, now in George Square, to
his numerous, if impermanent, family of brothers and
sisters, and to the High School.

As he grew up, his ill-health and weakness returned
and he was sent once more to stay in the Borders –
this time to Kelso, where he lived with an aunt, went
to the town school, and made the acquaintance there,
whether for good or ill, who shall say? of the
Ballantynes. And he had to return to Kelso for the same
reason at least once during his education. He did not

take the full usual number of courses, and did not excel at school. But he always read.

As it had not been decided which branch of the law he should pursue, he was apprenticed to his father at the age of fifteen, as a useful preparation for his career. He naturally enough did not enjoy preparing legal documents, but he did not go against his father's wishes by refusing to do it, and though signs of illness returned from time to time, his health was gradually improving and his strength increasing. This was partly, he thought, the result of taking long walks, a pastime in which he took great delight. He tried various accomplishments; but he could neither draw, nor make music, nor (at this time) write. Still he always read – irregularly, uncritically, but enormously, so that to this day Sir Walter's real learning is under-estimated. And he formed a very noteworthy circle of friends – William Clerk, 'Darsie Latimer', the chief of them all. It must have been just after he entered his father's office that he met Burns, during that poet's famous visit to Edinburgh in 1786–87.

Considerably less is known of his late youth and early manhood than of either his childhood or of his later life. His letters – those invaluable and unparalleled sources of biographical information – do not begin till 1792, the year in which he became of age, when, in July, he was called to the Bar. But it is widely believed that, in these years of apprenticeship, in more senses than one, he, partly in gratifying his own love of wandering, and partly in serving his father's business by errands to clients, etc., did more than lay the foundation of that unrivalled knowledge of Scotland, and of all classes in it, which plays so important a part in his literary work. Scott has been accused (for the most part foolishly) of paying an exaggerated respect to rank. But his familiarity with all ranks from an early age is undoubted, and only very shallow or prejudiced observers will doubt the beneficial effect which this had on his study of humanity.

The uneasy caricature which mars Dickens's picture of the upper, and even the upper middle, classes is as much absent from Scott's work as the complete want of familiarity with the lower which appears, for instance, in Bulwer. It is certain that before he had written anything, he was on familiar terms with many persons, both men and women, of the highest rank – the most noteworthy among his female correspondents being Lady Louisa Stuart (sister of the Marquis of Bute and granddaughter of Lady Mary Wortley Montagu) and Lady Abercorn. With the former, the correspondence was always simply on the footing of close friendship, literary and other. In his friendship with Lady Abercorn, there might have been a suspicion, especially on the lady's side, of that feeling:

> 'Too warm for friendship and too pure for
> love'

which undoubtedly sometimes does exist between men and women who cannot, and perhaps who would not if they could, turn love into marriage.

However this may be, let it be repeated that it is certain that Scott, from his fifteenth year, when he is said to have first visited the Highlands and seen Rob Roy's country, to his twenty-first birthday, and yet again in the five or six years between his call to the Bar and his marriage, visited many, if not all, parts of Scotland. He knew high and low, rich and poor, with the friendly interest of his temperament and the keen observation of his genius. He took part in business and amusement and conviviality (he admits in his later life to having been guilty of sharing in the prevalent tendency to drink rather heavily); and still and always *read*. He joined the 'Speculative Society' in January 1791, and, besides taking part in the debates on general subjects, read papers on Feudalism, Ossian, and Northern Mythology, in what were to be his more special lines.

His young lawyer friends called him 'Colonel Grogg', a nickname easy to understand given his confessed drinking habits, and 'Duns Scotus', which relates to his interest in history and Scotland; while yet a third characteristic, which can surprise nobody, is indicated in the famous introduction of him to a boisterous party of midshipmen of the Marryat type by James Clerk, the brother of Darsie Latimer, who kept a yacht, and was fond of the sea: 'You may take Mr Scott for a poor *lamiter*, gentlemen, but he is the first to begin a row and the last to end it'.

It appears that it was from a time somewhat before he was called to the Bar that the beginning of Scott's famous, his unfortunate, and (as many people have added, rightly or wrongly) his only love affair dates. Some persons have taken the trouble to piece together and eke out the references to 'Green Mantle', otherwise Miss Stuart of Belches, later Lady Forbes. It is better to respect Scott's own reticence on a subject of which very little is really known, and of which he, like most gentlemen, preferred to say little or nothing. The affection appears to have been mutual; but the lady was probably not very eager to incur family displeasure by making a match decidedly below her in rank, and, at that time, distinctly unwise for financial reasons. But the courtship, such as it was, appears to have been long, and the effects of the loss indelible. Scott speaks of his heart as 'handsomely pieced' – 'pieced', it may be observed, not 'healed'.

A healed wound sometimes does not show; a pieced garment or article of furniture reminds us of the piecing till the day when it goes to fire or dustbin. But it has been supposed, with some reason, that those heroines of Scott's who show most touch of personal sympathy – Catherine Seyton, Die Vernon, Lilias Redgauntlet – bear features, physical or mental or both, of this Astarte, this

'Lost woman of his youth, yet unpossessed.'

And no one can read the *Diary* without noticing the strange bitter-sweet, at the moment of his greatest calamity, of the fact that Sir William Forbes, who rendered him invaluable service at his greatest need, was his successful rival thirty years before, and the widower of 'Green Mantle'.

This affair came to an end in October 1796; and it may astonish some people, accustomed to thinking of Scott as a rather humdrum and prosaic person, who escaped the scandals so often associated with the memory of men of letters from sheer want of temptation, to hear that one of his most intimate friends of his own age at the time 'shuddered at the violence of his most irritable and ungovernable mind.' There is no reason to doubt the truth in this description. And those who know something of human nature might well attribute the disappearance of the irritableness and ungovernableness to the end of the affair, and to Scott's own strength of mind. Confronted by fate with the question whether he was to be the victim or the mas-

ter of his own passions, he fought out the battle once
and for all, and from then on guarded himself well
against the forces of passion. He may have lost something from it, but he also gained a great deal.

It has been said that he states (with a touch of irony,
no doubt) that his heart was 'handsomely pieced'; and it
does not contradict the theory given in the previous
paragraph, but instead gives the theory added weight,
that the piecing did not take long. In exactly a year,
Scott became engaged to Miss Charlotte Margaret Carpenter or Charpentier, and they were married on Christmas Eve, 1797, at St Mary's, Carlisle. They had met at
Gilsland Spa in the previous July, and the courtship had
not taken very long. The lady was of French extraction,
had an only brother in the service of the East India
Company, and, being an orphan, was the ward of the
Marquis of Downshire – circumstances on which gos-
sips like James Hogg made impertinent remarks. It is
fair, however, to 'the Ettrick Shepherd' to say that he
speaks enthusiastically both of Mrs Scott's appearance
('one of the most beautiful and handsome creatures I
ever saw in my life'; 'a perfect beauty') and of her character ('she is cradled in my remembrance, and ever shall
be, as a sweet, kind, and affectionate creature'). She was
very dark, small, with hair which Hogg calls black,
Lockhart dark brown; her features were not regular, but
her complexion, figure, and general appearance were

'unusually attractive'. Not very much is said about her in any of the authentic accounts, and traditional tittle-tattle may be neglected. She does not seem to have been extremely intelligent, and was not well-read; but neither of these defects precludes a happy marriage; and she was certainly a faithful and affectionate wife. At any rate, Scott made no complaints, if he had any to make, and nearly the most touching passage in the *Diary* is that written after her death.

The minor incidents, not literary, of his life, between his call to the Bar and his marriage, require a little attention, for they had a very great influence on the character of his future work. His success at the Bar was moderate, but his fees increased steadily if slowly. He defended (unsuccessfully) a Galloway minister who was accused among other counts of 'toying with a sweetie-wife', and it is interesting to find in his defence some casuistry about *ebrius* and *ebriosus*, which reminds one of the Baron of Bradwardine. He took part victoriously in a series of battles with sticks, between Loyalist advocates and writers and Irish Jacobin medical students, in the pit of the Edinburgh theatre during April 1794. In June 1795, he became a curator of the Advocates' Library, and a year later engaged (of course on the loyal side) in another great political 'row', this time in the streets.

Above all, in the spring and summer between the loss

of his love and his marriage, he engaged eagerly in volunteering, becoming quartermaster, paymaster, secretary, and captain in the Edinburgh Light Horse – an occupation which has left at least as much impression on his work as Gibbon's equally famous connection with the Hampshire Militia on his. His friendships continued and multiplied; and he began with the sisters of some of his friends, especially Miss Cranstoun (his chief confidante in the 'Green Mantle' business) and Miss Erskine, the first, or the first known to us, of those interesting correspondences with ladies which show him perhaps at his very best. For. in them, he plays neither jester, nor coxcomb, nor sentimentalist, nor any of the involuntary counterparts which men in such cases are too apt to play; and they contributed considerably to his rightly earning the great name of gentleman.

But by far the most important contribution of these six or seven years to his development was his increasing knowledge of the scenery, and customs, and traditions, and dialects, and local history of his own country, which his greater independence, enlarged circle of friends, and somewhat increased means enabled him to acquire. It is quite true that to a man with his gifts any microcosm will do for a macrocosm in miniature. He is said to have picked up the word 'whomled' – meaning 'bucketed over', 'turned like a tub', which adds so much to the description of the nautical misfortune of Claud Halcro

19

and Triptolemus in *The Pirate*, by overhearing it from a scold in the Grassmarket. But still the enlarged experience could not but be of the utmost value. It was during these years that he saw Glamis Castle in its unspoiled state, during these that, in connection with the case of the unfortunate but rather happily named devotee of Bacchus and Venus, McNaught, he explored Galloway, and obtained the decorations and scenery, if not the story, of *Guy Mannering*. He also repeated his visits to the English side of the Border, not merely on the occasion during which he met Miss Carpenter, but earlier, in a second excursion to Northumberland.

But, above all, these were the years of his famous 'raids' into Liddesdale, then one of the most inaccessible districts of Scotland, under the guidance of Mr Shortreed of Jedburgh – raids which completed the information for *Guy Mannering*, which gave him much of the material for the *Minstrelsy*, and the history of which has probably delighted every one of his readers and biographers, except one or two who have been scandalized at the exquisite story of the Arrival of the Keg. Of these let us not speak, but, regarding them with a tender pity not unmixed with wonder, pass to the beginnings of his actual literary life and to the history of his early married years. The literature a little preceded the life; but the life certainly determined the growth of the literature.

CHAPTER

II

$\mathscr{E}$ARLY LITERARY WORK

It is pretty universally known, and must have been perceived even from the foregoing summary, that Scott was by no means a very precocious writer. He takes rank, indeed, neither with those who, according to a famous phrase, 'break out threescore thousand strong' in youth; nor with those who begin writing original work early, and by degrees arrive at excellence; nor yet with those who do not display any literary talent till late in life. His class – a fourth, which, at least as regards the greater names of literature, is perhaps the smallest of all – comprises those who may almost be said to drift into literary work and literary fame, whose first production is not merely tentative and unoriginal, but, so to speak, accidental, who do not discover their real faculty for literary work till after a pretty long course of casual literary play.

Part of this was no doubt due to the fact that, according to reliable sources, Walter Scott the elder had, even more than his image the elder Fairford, that horror of literary employment on the part of his son which was for generations a tradition among the business classes. It was also due partly, perhaps, to a metaphysical cause – the fact that until Scott was well past his twentieth year, the wind of the spirit was not yet blowing and the new poetical and literary day had not yet dawned; and partly to a more commonplace reason or set of reasons. About 1790, literary work was extremely badly paid; and, even if it had been paid better, Scott had no particular need of money. Up to the time of his marriage he lived at home, spent his holidays with friends, or on tours where the expenses were little or nothing, and obtained sufficient pocket money, first by copying while he was still apprenticed to his father, then by his fees when he was called to the Bar.

He could, as he showed later, spend money royally when he had it (or thought he had it); but he was a man of no extravagant tastes of the ordinary kind, and Edinburgh was not in his days at all an extravagant place of living. Even when he married, he was by no means badly off. His wife, though not exactly an heiress, had means which had been estimated at five hundred a year, and which seem never to have fallen below two hundred; Scott's fees averaged about another two hundred; he evidently had an allowance from his father (who had been very well off, and was still not poor), and before very long the Sheriffship of Selkirkshire added three hundred more, though he seems to have made this an excuse for giving up practice, which he had never much liked. On his father's death in 1799, he inherited some property; legacies from relations added more. Before the publication of the *Lay* (when he was barely thirty-three), Lockhart estimates his income, leaving fees and literary work out of the question, at nearly if not quite a thousand a year; and a thousand a year at the beginning of the century went as far as fifteen hundred, if not two thousand, at its close.

Thus, with no necessity to live by his pen, with no immediate or extraordinary temptation to use it for gain, and as yet, it would seem, with no overwhelming compulsion from his genius to do so, while he at no time of his life felt any stimulus from vanity, it is not surprising that it was long before Scott began to write in earnest. A few childish verse translations and exercises of his neither encourage nor forbid any particular expectations of literature from him; they are neither better nor worse than those of hundreds, probably thousands, of boys every year.

His first published performance, now of extreme rarity, and not, of course, produced with any literary object, was his Latin call-thesis on the rather curious subject (which has been, not improbably, supposed to be connected with his German studies and the terror literature of the last decade of the century) of the disposal of the dead bodies of legally executed persons. His first English work was directly the result of the said German studies, to which, like many of his contemporaries, he had been attracted by fashion. It consisted of nothing more than the well-known translations of Bürger's *Lenore* and *Wild Huntsman*, which were issued in a little quarto volume by Manners & Miller of Edinburgh, in October 1796 – a date which has the special interest of suggesting that Scott sought some refuge in literature from the agony of his rejection by Miss Stuart.

These well-known translations, or rather imitations, the first published under the title of *William and Helen*, which it retains, the other as *The Chase*, which was subsequently altered to the better and more literal rendering, show unmistakably the result of the study of ballads, both in the printed forms and as orally delivered. Some crudities of rhyme and expression are said to have been corrected at the instance of one of Scott's (at this time rather numerous) Egerias (female advisors) the beautiful wife of his relative, Scott of Harden, a young lady partly of German extraction, but of the best English breeding. Slim books of this kind, even translations, made a great deal more mark sometimes in those days than they would in these; but there were a great many translations of *Lenore* about, and except by Scott's friends, little notice was taken of the volume. There were some excuses for the neglect, the best perhaps being that English criticism at the time was at nearly as low an ebb as English poetry. A really acute critic could hardly have mistaken the difference between Scott's verse and the fustian or tinsel of the Della Cruscans, the frigid rhetoric of Darwin, or the drivel of Hayley. Only Southey had as yet written ballad verses with equal vigour and facility; and he had not yet published any of them. It is Scott who tells us that he borrowed

> 'Tramp, tramp, along the land they rode,
> Splash, splash, along the sea.'

from Taylor of Norwich; but Taylor himself had the good taste to see how much it was improved by the completion

> 'The scourge is red, the spur drops blood,
> *The flashing pebbles flee.*'

Which last line, indeed, Coleridge himself hardly bettered in the not-yet-written *Ancient Mariner*, the ultimate example of the style. It must be mainly a question of individual taste whether the sixes and eights of the *Lenore* version or the continued eights of the *Huntsman* please most. But anyone who knows what the present state of British poetry was in October 1796 will appreciate the merits of either.

It was never Scott's way to be cast down at the failure or the neglect of any of his work; nor does he ever seem to have been moved by the more masculine but perhaps equally childish determination to 'do it again' and 'shame the fools'. It seems quite on the cards that he might have calmly accepted that he might never achieve recognition, and have continued as a mere literary lawyer, with a pretty turn of verse and a great amount of reading, if his most intimate friend, William Erskine, had not met 'Monk' Lewis in London, and found him anxious for contributions to his *Tales of Wonder*.

Lewis was a frivolous and vain man, and rather a snob: his *Monk* is not very clean fustian, and most of his other work rubbish. But he was, though it was not widely known, a sincere Romantic and he had no petty jealousy in literary matters. Above all, he had, as Scott recognized, but as has not been always recognized since, a really remarkable and then novel command of flowing but fairly strict lyrical measures, the very things needed to thaw the frost of the eighteenth-century couplet. Erskine offered, and Lewis gladly accepted, contributions from Scott, and though *Tales of Wonder* were much delayed, and did not appear till 1801, the project directly caused the production of Scott's first original work in ballad, *Glenfinlas* and *The Eve of St John*, as well as the less important pieces of the *Fire King*, *Frederick and Alice*, etc.

In *Glenfinlas* and *The Eve*, the real Scott first shows. *The Eve* is the better of the two works. There are several factors which contribute to its superiority. Firstly, although Scott had a great liking for and much proficiency in 'eights', that metre is never so effective for ballad purposes as eights and sixes. Secondly, *Glenfinlas* exhibits a Germanisation which is at the same time an adulteration. Thirdly, well as Scott knew the Perthshire Highlands, they could not appeal to him with the same subtle intimacy of touch as that possessed by the ruined-tower where, as a half paralysed infant, he had been herded with the lambs.

These three factors, and others, join to produce a freer effect in *The Eve*. The eighteenth century is farther off; the genuine medieval inspiration is nearer. And it is especially noticeable that, as in most of the early performances of the great poetical periods, an alteration of metrical etiquette (as we may call it) plays a great part. Scott had not yet heard that recitation of *Christabel* which had so great an effect on his work, and through it on the work of others. But he had mastered for himself, and by study of the originals, the secret of the *Christabel* metre, that is to say, the wide licence of equivalence in trisyllabic and dissyllabic feet, of metre catalectic or not, as need was, of anacrusis and the rest. As is natural to a novice, he rather exaggerates his liberties, especially in the cases where the internal rhyme seduces him. It is necessary not merely to slur, but to gabble, in order to get some of these into proper rhythm, while in other places the mistake is made of using so many anapaests that the metre becomes, not as it should be, iambic, with anapaests for variation, but anapaestic without even a single iamb. But these are 'sma' sums, sma' sums', as says his own Bailie Jarvie, and on the whole the required effect of vigour and variety, of narrative giving place to terror and terror to narrative is well achieved. Above all, in neither piece do we find anything of what the poet has so well characterized in one of his early reviews as the 'spurious style of tawdry and affected simplicity which trickles through the legendary ditties' of the eighteenth century. 'The hunt is up' in earnest; and we are chasing the tall deer in the open hills, not coursing rabbits with toy terriers on a bowling green.

The writing of these pieces had, however, been preceded by the publication of Scott's second volume, the translation of *Goetz von Berlichingen*, for which Lewis had arranged with a London bookseller, so that this time the author received his due reward. He received twenty-five guineas, and was to have as much more for a second edition, which the short date of copyright forestalled. The book appeared in February 1799, and received more attention than the ballads, though it was in fact belated, the brief English interest in German *Sturm und Drang* having ceased directly, though indirectly it gave Byron much of his hold on the public a dozen years later. At about the same time, Scott wrote, but did not publish, an original, or partly original, dramatic work of the same kind, *The House of Aspen*, which he contributed thirty years later to *The Keepsake*. Few good words have ever been said for this, and perhaps not many people have ever cared much for the *Goetz*, either in the original or in the translation. Goethe did not, in drama at least, understand adventurous matter, and Scott had no grasp of dramatic form.

It has been said that there was considerable delay in the publication of the *Tales of Wonder*; and some have discussed what direct influence this delay had on Scott's further and further advance into the waters of literature. It is certain that he at one time thought of publishing his contributions independently, and that he did actually print a few copies of them privately; and it is extremely probable that his little experiments in publication, mere *hors-d'oeuvres* as they were, had whetted his appetite. Even the accident of his friend Ballantyne's having taken to publishing a newspaper, and having room at his press for what printers profanely call 'job-work', may have had some influence. What is certain is that the project of editing a few Border ballads – a selection of his collection which might make 'a neat little volume of four or five shillings' – was formed roughly in the late autumn of 1799, and had taken very definite shape by

April 1800. Heber, the great bibliophile and brother of the Bishop, introduced Scott to that curious person Leyden, whose gifts, both original and erudite, are undoubted, although perhaps his exile and early death contributed to their fame. And it so happened that Leyden was both a lover of old ballads and a skilful composer of new. The impetuous Borderer pooh-poohed a 'thin thing' such as a four or five shilling book, and Scott, nothing loath, extended his project. Most of his spare time during 1800 and 1801 was spent on it; and besides corresponding with the man who 'fished this murex up', Bishop Percy, he entered into literary relations with Joseph Ritson. Even Ritson's waspish character seems to have been softened by Scott's courtesy, and perhaps even more by the joint facts that he had as yet attained no literary reputation, and neither at this nor at any other time gave himself literary airs. He also made the acquaintance of George Ellis, who became a warm and intimate friend. These were the three men of the day who, since Warton's death, knew most of early English poetry, and though Percy was too old to help, the others were not.

The scheme grew and grew, especially by the inclusion in it of the publication not merely of ballads, but of the romance of *Sir Tristrem* (of the authorship of which by someone else than Thomas the Rhymer, Scott never would be convinced), till the neat four or five shilling volume originally proposed was quite out of the question. When at last the two volumes of the first (Kelso) edition appeared in 1802, not merely was *Sir Tristrem* omitted, but a great deal else which, still without 'the knight who fought for England', subsequently appeared in a third. The earliest form of the *Minstrelsy of the Scottish Border* is a very pretty book; it deservedly established the fame of Ballantyne as a printer, and as it was not printed in the huge numbers that reduced the money value of Sir Walter's later books, is more vauable to the collector. The paper and type are excellent; the printing (with a few slips in the Latin quotations such as *concedunt* for *comedunt*) is very accurate, and the frontispiece, a view of Hermitage Castle in the rain, has the interest of presenting what is said to have been a very faithful view of the actual state of Lord Soulis' stronghold and the place of the martyrdom of Ramsay. This picture was produced in three curious stages; first, a drawing by Scott, who could not draw at all; second, a reworking by Clerk, who had never seen the place; and third, an engraving by an artist who was equally innocent of local knowledge.

The book, however, which brought in the modest profit of rather less than eighty pounds, would have had equal effect upon its public no matter how it was produced. The shock of Percy's *Reliques* was renewed, and in a far more favourable atmosphere, before a far better prepared audience. The public indeed had not yet been 'ground-baited' up to the consummation of thousands of copies of poetry as they were later by Scott himself and Byron; but an edition of eight hundred copies was sold in the course of the year, and a second, with the additional volume, was at once called for. It contained, indeed, not much original verse, though *Glenfinlas* and *The Eve*, with Leyden's *Cout of Keeldar*, *Lord Soulis*, etc., appeared in it after a fashion which Percy had set and Evans had continued.

But the ballads, familiar as they have become since, not merely in the *Minstrelsy* itself, but in a hundred fresh collections, selections, and what not, could never be mistaken by anyone fitted to appreciate them. *The Outlaw Murray*, with its rub-a-dub of e rhymes throughout, opens the book very cunningly, with something not of the best, but good enough to excite expectation – an expectation surely not to be disappointed by the immortal agony (dashed with one stroke of magnificent wrath) of *Helen of Kirkconnell*, the bustle, frolic, and battle-joy of the Border pieces proper, the solemn notes of *The Lyke-Wake Dirge*, the eeriness of *Clerk Saunders* and *The Wife of Usher's Well*.

Even Percy had not been lucky enough to hit upon anything so characteristic of the *average* ballad style at its best as the opening stanza of *Fause Foodrage*:

'King Easter courted her for her lands,
King Wester for her fee,
King Honour for her comely face
And for her fair bodie;'

And Percy would no doubt have been tempted to 'polish' such more than average touches, such as Margaret's 'turning', without waking, in the arms of her lover as he receives his deathblow, or as the incomparable stanza in *The Wife of Usher's Well* which tells how

'By the gates of Paradise
That birk grew fair eneugh.'

Those who study literature in what they are pleased to call a scientific manner have, as was to be expected, found fault with Scott (mildly or not, according to their degree of sense and taste), for the manner in which he edited these ballads. It may be admitted that the practice of mixing imitations with originals is a questionable one; and that in some other cases, Scott, though he was far from the illegitimate and tasteless fashion of alteration, of which in their different ways Allan Ramsay and Percy himself had set the example, was not always up to the highest lights on this subject of editorial faithfulness. It must, for instance, seem odd to most readers that he should have thought it proper to print Dryden's

33

Virgil with Dr Somebody's pedantic improvements instead of Dryden's own text. But the case of the ballads is very different. Here, it must be remembered, there is no authentic original at all. Even in the rare cases, where very early printed or manuscript copies exist, we not only do not know that these are the originals, we have every reasonable reason for being pretty certain that they are not. In the case of ballads taken down from repetition, we know as a matter of certainty that, according to the ordinary laws of human nature, the reciter has altered the text which he or she heard, that that text was in its day and way altered by someone else, and so on almost *ad infinitum*. 'Mrs Brown's version', therefore, or Mr Smith's, or Mr Anybody's, has absolutely no claims to sacrosanctity.

It is a good thing, no doubt, that all such versions should be collected by someone (as in this case by Professor Child) who had the means, the time, and the patience. But for the purposes of reading, for the purposes of poetic enjoyment, such a collection is nearly valueless. We must have it for reference, of course. But who can *read* a dozen versions, say, of *The Queen's Marie* with any pleasure? What is exquisite in one is watered, messed, spoiled by the others.

Therefore, although the most excellent way of all might have been to record his alterations, and the original, in an appendix – dustbin of *apparatus criticus* – Scott was right, and trebly right, in such dealing as that with the first stanza of *Fause Foodrage*. That stanza, as it stands above, does not occur in any of the extant quasi-originals. 'Mrs Brown's manuscript', from which, as Professor Child says, with almost silent reproach, Scott took his text, 'with some forty small changes', reads

> 'King Easter has courted her for her gowd,
> King Wester for her fee,
> King Honour for her lands sae braid,
> And for her fair bodie.'

Now this is clearly wrong. Either 'gowd' or 'lands' is a mere repetition of 'fee', and if not, the reading does not point any ethical antithesis between Kings Easter and Wester and their more chivalrous rival. As it happens, there are two other versions, shorter and less dramatic, but one of them distinctly giving, the other implying, the sense of Scott's alteration. Scott was quite justified in adjusting the one text that he did print, especially as he did it in his own right way, and not in the wrong one of Percy and Mickle. There is here no Bentleian impertinence, no gratuitous meddling with the at least possibly genuine text of a known and definite author. The editor simply picks out of the mud, and wipes clean, something precious, which has been defaced by bad usage, and has become masterless.

The third volume of the *Minstrelsy* was pretty speedily got ready, with more matter; and *Sir Tristrem* (which is in a way a fourth) was not very long in following. This last part contained a *tour de force* in the shape of a completion of the missing part by Scott himself, a completion which, of course, shocks philologists, but which was certainly never written for them, and possesses its own value for others.

Not the least part of the interest of the *Minstrelsy* itself was the editor's appearance as a prose writer. Percy had started, and others down to Ritson had continued, the practice of interspersing verse collections with dissertations in prose; and while the first volume of the *Minstrelsy* contained a long general introduction of more than a hundred pages, and most of the ballads had separate prefaces of more or less length, the preface to *Young Tamlane* turned itself into an written examination of fairy lore, which, being printed in small type, is probably not much shorter than the general introduction.

In these pieces (the 'fairy' essay is said to be based on information partly furnished by Leyden), all the well-known characteristics of Scott's prose style appear – its occasional incorrectness, from the strictly scholastic point of view, as well as its far more than counterbalancing merits of vivid presentation, of arrangement, not orderly in appearance but curiously effective in result, of multifarious facts and reading, of the bold pictorial vigour of its narrative, of its pleasant humour, and its incessant variety.

Nor was this the only opportunity that the earliest years of the century afforded to Scott for exercising himself in the medium which, even more than verse, was to be his. The *Edinburgh Review* was started in 1802. Although its politics were not Scott's, they were for some years much less violently put forward and exclusively enforced than was the case later; indeed, the *Review* started with much the same ostensible policy as the *Whig Deliverer* a century before, the policy, at least in declared intention, of using both parties as far as might be for the public good.

The attempt, if made in good faith, was not more successful in one case than in the other; but it at least permitted Tories to enlist under the blue and yellow banner. The standard-bearer, Jeffrey, moreover, was a very old, an intimate, and a never-quite-to-be-divorced friend of Scott's. At a later period, Scott's contributions to periodicals attained a standard of excellence which has been obscured by the fame of the poems and novels together, even more unjustly than the poems have been obscured by the novels alone. His reviews at this time on Southey's *Amadis*, on Godwin's *Chaucer*, on Ellis's *Specimens*, etc., are a little crude and amateurish, especially in the direction (well known, to those who have ever had to do with editing, as a besetting sin of novices) of substituting a mere account of the book, with a few expressions of like and dislike, for a grasped and reasoned criticism of it. But this is far less peculiar to them than those who have not read the early numbers of the great reviews may suppose. The fact is that Jeffrey himself, Sydney Smith, Scott, and others were only feeling for the principles and practice of reviewing, as they themselves later, and the brilliant second generation of Carlyle and Macaulay, De Quincey and Lockhart, were to carry it out. Perhaps the very best specimens of Scott's powers in this direction are the prefaces which he contributed much later and gratuitously to John Ballantyne's *Novelists' Library* – things which compare in quality to Johnson's *Lives* as examples of the combined arts of criticism and biography. At the time of which we speak, he was developing his talents in this direction as much as in others.

We must now look back a little, so as to give a brief sketch of Scott's domestic life, from his marriage until the publication of *The Lay of the Last Minstrel*, which, with that of *Waverley* and the crash of 1825–26, supplies the three turning-points of his career. After a very brief spell in lodgings (where the landlady was shocked at Mrs Scott's habit of sitting constantly in her drawing room), the young couple took up residence in South Castle Street. From here, not very long afterwards, they moved to the house – the famous No. 39 – in the northern division of the same street. This house was to be Charlotte's home for the rest of her Edinburgh life and Scott kept possession of it until, after the crash and the onset of serious ill-health, he could no longer afford a house in Edinburgh. Their first child was born on the 14 October 1798, but did not live many hours.

As was much more customary with Edinburgh residents, even of moderate means, than it had been for at least a century with Londoners, Scott, while his own income was still very modest, took a cottage at Lasswade in the neighbourhood. Here he lived during the summer for years; and in March 1799 he and his wife went to London, for the first time in his case since he had been almost a baby. His father died during this visit, after a painful breakdown, which is said to have suggested the touching particulars of the deathbed of Chrystal Croftangry's benefactor, and was repeated to some extent in Scott's own case.

His appointment to the Sheriff(depute)ship of Selkirkshire was made in December 1799, and the post paid, for light work, three hundred a year. It need not have interfered with even an active practice at the Bar had such fallen to him, and at first did not require him to take up even a partial residence. The Lord-Lieutenant, however, Lord Napier of Ettrick, insisted on this,

and though Scott rather resented a strictness which seems
not to have been universal, he had to comply. He did
not, however, do so at once, and during the last year of
the eighteenth century and the first two of the nineteenth, Lasswade and Castle Street were Scott's habitats,
with various radiations; while in the spring of 1803 he
and Mrs Scott repeated their visit to London and extended it to Oxford. It is not surprising to read his confession in sad days, a quarter of a century later, of the
'ecstatic feeling' with which he first saw this, the place
in all the island which was his spiritual home.

The same year saw the alarm of invasion which followed the resumption of hostilities after the armistice
of Amiens; and Scott's attention to his quartermastership,
which he still held, seems to have given Lord Napier
the idea that he was devoting himself, not only *tam Marti
quam Mercurio*, but to Mars rather at Mercury's expense.
Scott, however, was never fond of being dictated to, and
he and his wife were still at Lasswade when the
Wordsworths visited them in the autumn, though
Scott accompanied them to his sheriffdom on their
way back to Westmoreland. He had not yet wholly
given up practice, and though its rewards were not
great, they reached about this time, it would seem,
their maximum sum of £218, which, in the days of
his fairy-money, he must often have earned by a single morning's work.

Lord Napier, by no means improperly (for it was a legal requirement, though often evaded, that four months' residence per annum should be observed), persisted; and Scott, after a pleasing but impracticable dream of taking up his summer residence in the Tower of Harden itself, which was offered to him, took a lease of Ashestiel, a pleasant country house – 'a decent farmhouse', he calls it, in his usual way – the owner of which was his relation, and absent in India. The place was not far from Selkirk, on the banks of the Tweed and in the centre of the Buccleuch country. He seems to have settled there by the end of July 1804. The family, after leaving it for the late autumn session in Edinburgh, returned at Christmas, by which time *The Lay of the Last Minstrel*, though not actually published, was printed and ready. It was issued in the first week of the new year 1805, and was, except Wordsworth's and Coleridge's, the first book published, which was distinctly and originally characteristic of the new poetry of the nineteenth century.

CHAPTER

III

THE VERSE ROMANCES

Although Scott was nearly thirty-four year when the *Lay* appeared, and although he had already a considerable literary reputation in Edinburgh, and some in London, the amount of his original publications was at that time small. Indeed, on the austere principles of those who deny 'originality' to such things as reviews, or as the essays in the *Minstrelsy*, it must be limited to a mere handful, though very pleasing; the half dozen of ballads made up by *Glenfinlas*, *The Eve of St John*, the rather inferior *Fire King*, the beautiful *Cadzow Castle* (not yet mentioned, but containing some of its author's most charming *topic* lines), the fragment of *The Grey Brother*, and a few minor pieces.

With the *Lay* he took an entirely different position. The mere bulk of the poem was considerable; and, putting aside for the instant its peculiarities of subject, metre, and general treatment, it was a daring innovation in point of class. The eighteenth century had, even under its own laws and conditions, distinctly eschewed long narrative poems, the unreadable epics of Glover, for instance, belonging to that class of exception which really does prove the rule. Pope's *Rape* had been burlesque, and his *Dunciad*, satire; hardly the ghost of a narrative had appeared in Thomson and Young; Shenstone, Collins, Gray, had written nothing of any length; the entire poetical works of Goldsmith probably do not exceed in length a canto of the *Lay*; Cowper had never attempted narrative; Crabbe was resting on the early laurels of his brief *Village*, etc., and had not begun his tales. *Thalaba*, indeed, had been published, and no doubt was not without effect on Scott himself; but it was not popular, and the author was still under the sway of the craze against rhyme. To all intents and purposes, the poet was addressing the public, in a work combining the attractions of fiction with the attractions of verse at considerable length, for the first time since Dryden had done so in his *Fables*, a hundred and five years before. And though the mastery of the method might be less, the stories were original, they were continuous, and they displayed an entirely new taste and seasoning both of subject and of style.

There can be no doubt at all, for those who put metre in its proper place, that a very large, perhaps the much larger, part of the appeal of the *Lay* was metrical. The public was sick of the couplet – had indeed been sickened twice over, if the abortive revolt of Gray and Collins be counted. It did not take, and was quite right in not taking, to the rhymeless, shortened Pindaric of Sayers and Southey, as to anything but an eccentric 'sport' of poetry. What Scott had to offer was practically new, or at least novel.

It is universally known – and Scott, who was only too careless of his own claims, and the very last of men to steal or conceal those of others, made no secret of it – that the suggestion of the *Lay* in metre came from a private recitation or reading of Coleridge's *Christabel*, written in the year of Scott's marriage, but not published till twenty years later, and more than ten after the appearance of the *Lay*. Coleridge seems to have regarded Scott's priority with an irritability less suitable to his philosophic than to his poetical character. But he had, in the first place, only himself, if anybody, to blame; in the second, Scott more than made the loan his own property by the variations executed on its motive; and in the third, Coleridge's original right was far less than he seems to have honestly thought, and than most people have guilelessly assumed since.

For the iambic dimeter, freely altered by the licences of equivalence, anacrusis, and catalexis, though not recently practised in English when *Christabel* and the *Lay* set the example, is an inevitable result of the clash between accented, alliterative, asyllabic rhythm and quantitative, exactly syllabic metre, which accompanied the transformation of Anglo-Saxon into English. We have distinct approaches to it in the thirteenth-century *Genesis*; it attains considerable development in Spenser's *The Oak and the Brere*; anybody can see that the latter part of Milton's *Comus* was written under the breath of its spirit. But it had not until this time been applied on any great scale, and the delusions under which the eighteenth century laboured as to the syllabic restrictions of English poetry had made it almost impossible that it should be. At the same time, that century, by its lighter practice on the one hand in the octosyllable, on the other in the four-footed anapaestic, was making the way easier for those who dared a little: and Coleridge first, then Scott, did the rest.

We have seen that in some of his early ballad work Scott had a little overdone the licence of equivalence, but this had probably been one of the formal points on which, as we know, the advice of Lewis, no poet but a remarkably good metrist, had been of use to him. And he acquitted himself now in a manner which, if it never quite attains the weird charm of *Christabel* itself at its best, is more varied, better sustained, and, above all, better suited to the story-telling which was, of course, Scott's supremest gift. It is very curious to compare Coleridge's remarks on Scott's verse with those of Wordsworth, in reference to the *White Doe of Rylstone*. Neither in *Christabel*, nor in the *White Doe*, is there a real *story* really told. Coleridge, but for his fatal weaknesses, undoubtedly could have told such a story; it is pretty certain that Wordsworth could not. But Scott could tell a story as few other men who have ever drawn breath on the earth could tell it. He had been distinguished in the conversational branch of the art from his youth up, and though it was to be long before he could write a story in prose, he showed now, at the first attempt, how he could write one in verse.

Construction, of course, was not his forte; it never was. The plot of the *Lay*, if not exactly non-existent, is of the simplest and loosest description; the whole being in effect a series of episodes strung together by the loves of Margaret and Cranstoun and the misdeeds of the Goblin Page. Even the Book supplies no real or necessary *nexus*. But the romance proper has never required elaborate construction, and has very rarely, if ever, received it. A succession of engaging or exciting episodes, each plausibly joined to the next, is sufficient for its purposes; and such a succession is liberally provided here.

So, too, it does not require strict character drawing – a gift with which Scott was indeed amply provided, but which he did not exhibit, and had no call to exhibit, here. If the characters will play their parts, that is enough. And they all play them very well here, though the hero and heroine do certainly exhibit something of that curious lack of strength which has been seen in the heroes nearly always, the heroines too frequently, of the later prose novels.

But even those critics who, as too many critics are wont to do, forgot and forget that 'the prettiest girl in the world' not only cannot give, but ought not to be asked to give, more than she has, must have been, and must be, very unreasonable if they find fault with the subject and stuff of the *Lay*. Jeffrey's remark about 'the present age not enduring' the Border and mass trooping details was contradicted by the fact, and was, as a matter of taste, one of those strange blunders which diversified his often admirably acute critical utterances. When he feared their effects on '*English* readers', he showed himself, as was not common with him, actually ignorant of one of the simplest general principles of the poetic appeal, that is to say, the element of *strangeness*. But we must not criticize criticism here, and must only add that another great appeal, that of variety, is amply given, as well as that of unfamiliarity.

The graceful and touching, if a little conventional, overture of the Minstrel introduces with the truest art the vigorous sketch of Branksome Tower. The spirits of flood and fell are allowed to impress and not allowed to bore us; for the quickest of changes is made to Deloraine's ride – a kind of thing in which Scott never failed, even in his latest and saddest days. The splendid Melrose opening of the Second Canto supports itself through the discovery of the Book, and finds due contrast in the description (or no-description) of the lovers' meeting; the fight and the Goblin Page's misbehaviour and punishment (to all, at least, but those, surely few now, who are troubled by the Jeffreyan sense of 'dignity'), the decoying and capture of young Buccleuch, and the warning of the clans are certainly no ungenerous provision for the Third; nor the clan anecdotes (especially the wonderful episode of the Beattisons), the parley, the quarrel of Howard and Dacre, and the challenge, for the Fourth. There is perhaps less in the Fifth, for Scott seems to have been afraid of another fight in detail; but the description of the night before, and the famous couplet,

> 'I'd give the lands of Deloraine
> Dark Musgrave were alive again.'

would save it if there were nothing else, as there is much. And if the actual conclusion has no great interest (Scott was never good at conclusions, as we shall find Lady Louisa Stuart telling him frankly later), the Sixth Canto is full, and more than full, of brilliant things – the feast, the Goblin's tricks, his carrying-off, the pilgrimage, and, above all, the songs, especially *Rosabelle* and the version of the *Dies Iræ*.

48

In similar fashion, he varies the rhymes, passing as the subject or the accompaniment of the word-music may require, from the couplet to the quatrain, and from the quatrain to the irregularly rhymed 'Pindaric'; always, however, taking care that, except in the set lyric, the quatrain shall not fall too much into definite stanza, but be interlaced in sense or sound sufficiently to carry on the narrative. The result, to some tastes, is a medium quite unsurpassed for the particular purpose. The only objection to it at all capable of being maintained, is that the total effect is rather lyrical than epic. And so much of this must be perhaps allowed as comes to granting that Scott's verse-romance is rather a long and cunningly sustained and varied ballad than an epic proper.

The *Lay*, though not received with quite that eager appetite for poetry which Scott was 'born to introduce', and of which he lived long enough to see the glutting, had a large and immediate sale. The author, not yet aware what a gold mine his copyrights were, parted with this after the first edition, and received in total less than £770, a small amount in comparison with his later gains; but probably the largest that had as yet been received by any English poet for a single volume not published by sub-scription. It is curious that, at the estimated rate of three for one in comparing the value of money at the end of the seventeenth and the beginning of the nineteenth century, the sum almost exactly equals that paid by

Tonson for Dryden's *Fables*, the last book, before the *Lay* itself, which had united popularity, merit, and bulk in English verse. But Dryden was the acknowledged head of English literature at the time, and Scott was a mere beginner. He was probably even better pleased with the quality of the praise than with the quantity of the pudding. For though professional criticism, then in no very vigorous state, said some silly things, it was generally favourable; and a saying of Pitt (most indifferent, as a rule, of all Prime Ministers to English literature) is memorable not merely as summing up the general impression, but as defining what that impression was in a fashion quite invaluable to the student of literary history. The Pilot that Weathered the Storm, it seems, said of the description of the Minstrel's hesitation before playing, 'This is a sort of thing I might have expected in painting, but could never have fancied capable of being given by poetry.'

The publication of the *Lay* immediately preceded, and perhaps its success had no small share in deciding, the most momentous and unfortunate step of Scott's life, his entry into partnership with James Ballantyne. The discussion of the whole of this business will best be postponed till the date of its catastrophe is reached, but a few words may be said on the probable reasons for it. Much, no doubt, was the result of that combination of incalculable things which foolish persons of one kind call mere chance, of which foolish persons of another kind deny the existence, and which wise men term, from different but not irreconcilable points of view, Providence, or Luck, or Fate. But a little can be cleared up. Scott had evidently made up his mind that he should not succeed at the Bar, and had also persuaded himself that the very success of the *Lay* had made failure certain. The ill success of his brother Thomas, with the legal business inherited from their father, perhaps inconvenienced and no doubt frightened him. In fact, though his harsher judges are wrong in attributing to him any undue haste to be rich, he certainly does seem to have been under a dread of being poor; a dread no doubt not wholly understandable and partly morbid in a young man still under thirty-five, with brilliant literary and some legal prospects, who had, independently of fees, literary or legal, a secured income of about a thousand a year.

He probably thought, and was right in thinking, that the book trade was going to 'look up' to a degree previously unknown; he seems throughout to have been under one of those inexplicable attractions towards the Ballantynes which now and then exist, as Hobbes says, 'in the greater towards the meaner, but not contrary'; and perhaps there was another cause which has not been usually allowed for enough. Good Christian and good-natured man as he was, Scott was exceedingly proud;

and though joining himself with persons of dubious social position in mercantile operations seems an odd way of pride, it had its temptations. Without doubt, from the first instance, Scott intended, more or less vaguely and dimly, to extend the printing business into a publishing one, and so to free himself from any necessity of going cap-in-hand to publishers.

However, for good or for ill, for this reason or for that, the partnership was formed, at first indirectly by way of loan, then directly by further advance on security of a share in the business, and finally so that Scott became, though he did not appear, the leading partner. And the very first letter that we have of his about the business shows the fatal flaw which he, the soul of honour, seems never to have detected till too late, if even then. The scheme for an edition of Dryden was already afloat, and the first editor proposed was a certain Mr Foster, who 'howled about the expense of printing'.

I still, says Scott to Ballantyne, *stick to my answer that I know nothing of the matter, but that, settle it how he and you will, it must be printed by you or be no concern of mine. This gives you an advantage in driving the bargain.*

Perhaps; but how about the advantage to Mr Foster of being advised by Ballantyne's partner to employ Ballantyne, while he was innocent of the knowledge of the identity of partner and adviser, and was even told that Scott 'knew nothing of the matter'?

Even before the quarrel, which soon occurred with Constable, established the Ballantynes – nominally the other brother, John – as publishers, Scott had begun, and was constantly pressing upon the different publishing houses with which he was connected, a variety of literary schemes of the most ambitious and costly character. All these books were to be printed by Ballantyne, and many of them edited by himself; while, when the direct publishing business was added, there was no longer any check on this dangerous proceeding.

It is most curious how Scott, the shrewdest and sanest of men in the vast majority of affairs, seems to have lost his head wherever books or lands were concerned. Himself both a lover of history and an historian, as well as a lover of literature, he seems to have taken it for granted that the same combination of tastes existed in the public to an extent which would pay all expenses, however lavishly incurred. To those who know how cold a face publishers turn on what others might call really interesting schemes, and how often these schemes, even when fostered, miscarry or barely pay expenses, it is not so surprising that some of Scott's schemes never got into being at all, and that others were dead losses.

His *Dryden*, an altogether admirable book, on which he lavished labour, and great part of which appealed to a still dominant prestige, may just have carried the editor's relatively modest fee of forty guineas a volume, or about £750 for the whole. But when one reads of twice that sum paid for the *Swift*, of £1,300 for the thirteen quartos of the *Somers Papers*, and so forth, the feeling is not that the sums paid were at all too much for the work done, but that the publishers must have been very lucky men if they ever saw their money again. The two first of these schemes certainly, the third perhaps, deserved success; and still more so did a great scheme for the publication of the entire *British Poets*, to be edited by Scott and Campbell, which indeed fell through in itself, but resulted indirectly in Campbell's excellent *Specimens* and Chalmers's invaluable if not very comely *Poets*. Even another project, a *Corpus Historicorum*, would have been magnificent, though it could hardly have been bookselling war. But the *Somers Tracts* themselves, the *Memoirs* and papers of Sadler, Slingsby, Carleton, Cary, etc., were of the class of book which requires subvention of some kind to prevent it from being a dead loss; and when the preventive check of the unwillingness of publishers was removed by the fatal establishment of *John* Ballantyne & Co, things became worse still.

There are few better instances of the eternal irony of fate than that the author of the admirable description of the bookseller's horror at Mr Pembroke's Sermons should have permitted, should have positively caused, the publishing at what was in effect his own risk, or rather his own certainty of loss, not merely of Weber's ambitious *Beaumont and Fletcher*, but of collections of *Tixall Poetry*, *Histories of the Culdees*, Wilson's *History of James the First*, and the rest.

As the beginning of 1805 saw the first birth of his real books, so the end of it saw that of the last of his children. His firstborn, as has been said, did not live. But Walter (born November 1799), Sophia (born October 1801), Anne (born February 1803), and Charles (born December 1805) survived infancy; and it is quite probable that these regular increases to his family, by suggesting that he might have a large one, stimulated Scott's desire to enlarge his income. As a matter of fact, however, the quartette of two boys and two girls was not exceeded.

The domestic life at Castle Street and Ashestiel, from the publication of the *Lay* to that of *Marmion* in 1808 – indeed to that of *The Lady of the Lake* in May 1810 – ran smoothly enough; and there can be little doubt that these five years were the happiest, and in reality the most prosperous, of Scott's life. He had at once attained great fame, and was increasing it by each successive poem; his immense intellectual activity found vent besides in almost innumerable projects, some of which were in a way successful, and some of which, if they did not bring him any personal gain, did good to more or less deserving friends and *protégés*. His health had, as yet, shown no signs whatever of breaking down. He was physically in perfect condition for, and at Ashestiel he had every opportunity of indulging in, the field sports in which he took at least as much pleasure as in reading and writing. He had time to indulge in travel; and, to crown it all, he was, during this period, in prospect of gaining a post earning him an income which should have put even his anxieties at rest, and which certainly might have made him dissociate himself from the dangerous and doubtful commercial enterprises in which he had engaged. This post was that of a Clerkship of Session, one of an honourable, well-paid, and by no means laborious group of offices which seem to have been accepted as comfortable situations for advocates of ability, position, and influence, who, for one reason or another, were not making absolutely first-rate mark at the Bar.

The post to which Scott was appointed was in the possession of a certain Mr Hope, and as no retiring pension was attached to these places, it was customary to hold them on the rather uncomfortable terms of doing the work till the former holder died, without getting any money. But before many years had passed, a pension scheme was put in operation; Mr Hope took his share of it, and Scott began to earn thirteen hundred a year in addition to his Sheriffship and to his private property, without taking any account at all of literary gains. The appointment had not actually been completed, though the patent had been signed, when the Fox and Grenville Government came in, and it so happened that the document had been so made out as to have enabled Scott, if he chose, to draw the whole salary and leave his predecessor in the cold. But this was soon set right.

In the visit to London which he paid (apparently for the purpose of getting the error corrected), he made the acquaintance of the unlucky Princess of Wales, who was at this time rather a favourite with the Tories. And when he came back to Scotland, the trial of Lord Melville gave him an opportunity of distinguishing himself by displaying a natural and understandable partisanship, which aggrieved his Whig friends. Politics in Edinburgh ran very high during this short break in the long Tory domination, and from it dates a story, to some minds, perhaps, one of the most interesting of all those about Scott, and connected indelibly with the scene of its occurrence.

It tells how, as he was coming down the Mound with Jeffrey and another Whig, after a discussion in the Faculty of Advocates on some proposals of innovation, Jeffrey tried to laugh the difference off, and how Scott, usually stoical enough, save in point of humour, broke out with actual tears in his eyes, 'No, no! it is no laughing matter. Little by little, whatever your wishes may be, you will destroy and undermine until nothing of what makes Scotland Scotland shall remain!'

During 1806 and 1807, the main occupations of Scott's leisure (if he can ever be said to have had such a thing) were the *Dryden* and *Marmion*. The latter of these appeared in February and the former in April 1808, a perhaps unique example of an original work, and one of criticism and compilation, both of unusual bulk and excellence, appearing, with so short an interval, from the same pen.

As for *Marmion*, it is surely by far the greatest, taking all constituents of poetical greatness together, of Scott's poems. It was not helped at the time, and probably never has been helped, by the author's plan of prefixing to each canto introductions of very considerable length, each addressed to one or other of his chief literary friends, and having little or nothing at all to do with the subject of the tale. Contemporaries complained that the main poem was thereby intolerably interrupted; posterity has taken the line of ignoring the introductions altogether. This is a very great pity, for not only do they contain some of Scott's best and oftenest quoted lines, but each is a really charming piece of occasional verse, and something more, in itself. The beautiful description of Tweedside in late autumn, the dirge on Nelson, Pitt, and Fox (which last, of course, infuriated Jeffrey), and, above all, the splendid passage on the *Morte d'Arthur* (which Scott had at this time thought of editing, but gave up to Southey) adorn the epistle to Rose; the picture of Ettrick Forest in that to Marriott is one of the best sustained things the poet ever did; the personal interest of the Erskine piece is of the highest, though it has fewer 'purple' passages, and it is well-matched with that to Skene; while the fifth to Ellis and the sixth and last to Heber nobly complete the batch. Only, though the things in this case *are* both rich and rare,

'We wonder what the devil they do there.'

Lockhart unearthed what Scott seems to have forgotten, the fact that they were originally intended to appear by themselves. It is a pity they did not; for, excellent as they are, they are quite out of place as interludes to a story.

In *Marmion*, while Scott had lost little, if anything, of the formal graces of the *Lay*, he had improved immensely in grip and force. Clare may be a bread-and-butter heroine, and Wilton a milk-and-water lover, but the designs of Marmion against both give a real story interest, which is quite absent from the *Lay*. The figure of Constance is really tragic, not melodramatic merely, and makes one regret that Scott, in his prose novels, did not repeat and vary her. All the accessories, both in incident and figure, are good, and it is almost superfluous to praise the last

60

canto. It extorted admiration from the partisan rancour and the literary prudishness of Jeffrey; it made the disturbed dowagers of the *Critical Review*, who thought, with Rymer, that 'a hero ought to be virtuous', mingle applause with their complaints; it has been the delight of every reader ever since. The last canto of *Marmion* and the last few 'Aventiuren' of the *Nibelungen Lied* are perhaps the only things in all poetry where a set continuous battle (not a series of duels as in Homer) is related with unerring success; and the steady *crescendo* of the whole, considering its length and intensity, is really miraculous.

Indeed, even without this astonishing finale, the poem that contained the opening sketch of Norham, the voyage from Whitby to Holy Island, the final speech of Constance, and the famous passage of her knell, the Host's Tale, the pictures of Crichton and the Blackford Hill view, the 'air and fire' of the 'Lochinvar' song, the phantom summons from the Cross of Edinburgh, and the parting of Douglas and Marmion, could spare half of these and still remain one of the best of its kind, while every passage so spared would be enough to distinguish any poem in which it occurred.

The considerable change in the metre of *Marmion* as compared with the *Lay* is worth noticing. Here, as there, the 'introductions' are, for the most part, if not throughout, in continuous octosyllabic couplets. But, in the text, the couplet plays also a much larger part than it does in the *Lay*, and where it is dropped the substitute is not usually the light and extremely varied medley of the earlier poem, so much as a sort of irregular (and sometimes almost regular) stanza arrangement, sets of (usually three) octosyllables being interspersed with sixes, rhyming independently. The batches of monorhymed octosyllables sometimes extend to even four in number, with remarkably good effect, as, for instance, in the infernal proclamation from the Cross. Altogether the metrical scheme is more sombre than that of the *Lay*, and suits the more serious and tragic tone of the story.

It has been mentioned above in passing that Jeffrey reviewed *Marmion* on the whole unfavourably. The story of this review is well known: how the editor reviewer (with the best intentions doubtless) sent the proof with a kind of apology to Scott on the morning of a dinner-party in Castle Street; how Scott showed at least outward indifference, and Mrs Scott a not unamiable petulance; and how, though the affair caused no open breach of private friendship, it doubtless gave help to the increasing Whiggery of the *Review* and its pusillanimous policy in regard to the Spanish War in severing Scott's connection with it, and determining him to promote, heart and soul, the opposition venture of the *Quarterly*. It was naturally enough proposed by Canning that Scott should be editor of the *Quarterly*; but, as naturally, he does not seem to have even considered the proposal. He would have hated living in London; no salary that could have been offered him could have bettered, or even equalled, the stipends of his Sheriffship and the coming Clerkship, which he would have had to give up. The work would have interfered much more seriously than his actual vocations with his literary avocations. Besides, it is quite certain that he would not have made a good editor. In the first place, he was fitted neither by education nor by temperament for the troublesome and meticulous business of knocking contributions into shape. And, in the second, he would undoubtedly have fallen into the most fatal of all editorial errors – that of inserting articles, not because they were actually good or likely to be popular, but because the subjects were interesting, or the writers agreeable, to himself. But he backed the venture manfully with advice, by recruiting for it, and afterwards by contributing to it.

It so happened, too, that about the same time he had disagreements with the publisher as well as with the editor of the *Edinburgh Review*. Constable, though he had not entered into the intimate relations with Scott and the Ballantynes that were afterwards so fatal, had made the spirited bid of a thousand pounds for *Marmion*, and the much more spirited and (it is to be feared) much less profitable one of fifteen hundred for the *Swift*. He had, however, recently taken into partnership a certain Mr Hunter of Blackness. This Hunter must have had some merits – he had at any rate sufficient wit to throw the blame of the fact that sojourn in Scotland did not always agree with Englishmen on their disgusting habit of 'eating too much *and not drinking enough*.' But he was a laird of some family, and he seems to have thought that he might bring into business the slightly hectoring ways which were then tolerated in Scotland from persons of quality to persons of none or less. He was a very bitter Whig, and, therefore, ill disposed towards Scott. And, lastly, he had, or thought he had, a grievance against his distinguished 'hand' in respect of the *Swift*, to wit, that the editor of that well-paid compilation did not devote himself to it by any means exclusively enough.

Now Scott, though the most good-natured of men and only too easy to lead, was absolutely impossible to drive; and his blood was as ready as the 'bluid of McFoy' itself to be set on fire at the idea of a cock-laird from Fife not merely treating a Scott with discourtesy, but accusing him of dubious conduct. He offered to throw up the *Swift*, and though this was not accepted, broke for a time all other connection with Constable – an unfortunate breach, as it helped to bring about the establishment of the Ballantyne publishing business, and so unquestionably began Scott's own ruin. It is remarkable that a similar dislike of interference afterwards broke Scott's just-begun connection with Blackwood, which, could it have lasted, would probably have saved him. For that wise person would certainly never have plunged, or, if he could have helped it, let anyone else plunge, into Charybdis.

Between the publication of *Marmion* and that of *The Lady of the Lake* Scott was very busy in bookmaking and bookselling projects. It was characteristic of the mixture of bad luck and bad management which hung on the Ballantynes from the first that even their *Edinburgh Annual Register*, published as it was in the most stirring times, and written by Scott, by Southey, and others of the very best hands, was a failure. Scott made some visits to London, and (for the scenery of the new poem) to the Trossachs and Loch Lomond.

During this time he also faced some matters of family concern, the chief of which were the death of his famous bull-terrier Camp, and two troublesome affairs connected with his brothers. One of these, the youngest, Daniel, after misconduct of various kinds, had, as mentioned above, been guilty of cowardice during a Negro insurrection in Jamaica, and so disgusted his brother that when he came home to die, Scott would neither see him, nor, when he died, go to his funeral. The other concerned his brother Thomas, who, after his failure as a lawyer, had gone to the Isle of Man, where he for a time was an officer in the local Fencibles. But before leaving Edinburgh, and while he was still a practising lawyer, his brother had appointed him to a small post in his own gift as Clerk. Not only was there nothing discreditable in this according to the idea of any time – for Thomas Scott's education and profession qualified him fully for the office – but there were circumstances which, at that time, showed rather heroic and uncommon virtue.

For the actual vacancy had occurred in a higher and more valuable post, also in Scott's gift, and Scott, instead of appointing his brother to this, promoted a deserving subordinate veteran, and gave the lower and less valuable place to Thomas. Thomas's circumstances, however, obliged him to perform his duties by deputy, and a Commission sitting at the time ultimately abolished the office altogether, with a retiring allowance of about half the salary. Certain Whig peers took this up as a cause, and Lord Lauderdale, supported by Lord Holland, made in the House of Lords very offensive charges against Scott personally for having appointed his brother to a place which he knew would be abolished, and against Thomas for claiming compensation in respect of duties which he had never performed. The Bill was, however, carried; but Scott was indignant at the loss threatened to his brother and the imputation made on himself, and shunned Lord Holland at a semi-public dinner not long afterwards. For this he was and has since been severely blamed, and his behaviour was perhaps a little extreme. But everybody knows, or should know, that there are few things more trying to a man than to be accused of improper conduct when he believes himself to have behaved with unusual and saint-like propriety.

The Lady of the Lake appeared in May 1810, being published by Ballantyne and Miller, and at once became enormously popular. Twenty thousand copies were sold within the year, two thousand of which were costly quartos; and while there can be no doubt that this was the highest point of Scott's poetical vogue, it is probably generally accepted that the poem has always continued to be a greater favourite with the general readership than any other of his. More than any other, this poem created the passion for Scottish scenery and touring which lives in people at home and abroad to this day. It supplied in the descriptions of that scenery, in the fight between Roderick and Fitz-James, and in other things, his most popular passages; and it is probably considered, by most of his readers, to be the model poem of all his poetry.

Yet there are some who like it less than any other of the major divisions of that poetry, and this is not necessarily due either to a desire to be eccentric or to the subtler but almost equally illegitimate operation of the want of novelty – of the fact that its best effects are only repetitions of those of *Marmion* and the *Lay*. For, fine as it is, it seems to display the drawbacks of Scott's scheme and method more than any of the longer poems. Douglas, Ellen, Malcolm, are null; Roderick and the king have a touch of theatricality which is not found elsewhere in Scott; there is nothing fantastic in the piece like the Goblin Page, and nothing tragical like Constance. There is something teasing in what has been profanely called the 'guide-book' character – the cicerone-like fidelity which contrasts so strongly with the skilfully subordinated description in the two earlier and even in the later poems. Moreover, though Ellis ought not to have called the octosyllable 'the Hudibrastic measure' (which is only a very special variety of it), he was certainly right in objecting to its great predominance in unmixed form here.

The critics, however, sang the praises of the poem lustily. Even Jeffrey – perhaps because it was purely Scottish (he had thought *Marmion* not Scottish enough), perhaps because its greater conventionality appealed to him, perhaps because he wished to make atonement – was extremely complimentary. And certainly no one need be at a loss for things to praise positively, whatever may be his comparative estimate. The fine Spenserian openings (which Byron copied almost slavishly in the form of the stanza he took for *Harold*), the famous beginning of the stag, the description of the pass (till Fitz-James begins to soliloquize), some of the songs (especially the masterly 'Coronach'), the passage of the Fiery Cross, the apparition of the clan (not perhaps so great as some have thought it, but still great), the struggle, the guardroom (which shocked Jeffrey dreadfully) – these are only some of the best things. But the best of them is not equal to the last stand of the spearmen at Flodden, and the unburying of the Book in the *Lay*.

In order to complete the outline of Scott's verse romances in this chapter, it is necessary to look further ahead in his life; for not very long after the publication of the *Lady of the Lake*, Scott resumed the writing of *Waverley*, which brought about a complete change in the direction of his literature; and it was less than a year later that he planned the establishment at Abbotsford, which was from then on the headquarters of his life.

The first poem to follow was one which stood apart from the series in subject, scheme, and dress, and which perhaps should rather be counted with his minor and miscellaneous pieces – *The Vision of Don Roderick*. It was written quite speedily, even for him, and with a special purpose. The profits were promised in advance to the Committee of the Portuguese Relief Fund, formed to assist the sufferers from Massena's devastations. It consists of less than a hundred Spenserian stanzas, the story of Roderick merely ushering in a magical revelation, to that too-amorous monarch, of the fortunes of the Peninsular War and its heroes up to the date of writing. The *Edinburgh Review*, which hated the war, was very angry because Scott did not celebrate Sir John Moore (whether as a good Whig or a bad general it did not explain); but even Jeffrey was not entirely unfavourable, and the piece was otherwise well received. The description of the subterranean hall beneath the Cathedral of Toledo is as good as any reader might expect, and the verses on Saragossa and on the forces of the three kingdoms are very fine. But the whole was something of a *torso*, and it is improbable that Scott could ever have used the Spenserian stanza to good effect for continuous narrative. Even in its individual shape, that great form requires the artistic patience as well as the natural gift of men like its inventor, or like Thomson, Shelley, and Tennyson, in other times and of other schools, to get the full effect out of it; while to connect it satisfactorily with its kind and adjust it to narrative is harder still.

The true successor to his previous poetical works, however, after this parenthesis, was *Rokeby*, which was dated on the very last day of 1812. Its reception was not terribly enthusiastic; for Byron, borrowing most of his technique and general scheme from Scott, and adding to these a greater apparent passion and a more novel and unfamiliar local colour, had appeared on the scene as a 'second lion'. The public, a 'great-sized monster of ingratitudes', had got accustomed to Scott, if not weary of him. The title was not very happy; and perhaps some harm was really done by one of the best of Moore's many good jokes in the *Twopenny Postbag*, where he represented Scott as coming from Edinburgh to London,

'To do all the gentlemen's seats by the way'

in romances of half a dozen cantos.

The poem, however, is a very delightful one, and to some tastes at least far more worthy than the *Lady of the Lake*. Scott, indeed, clung to the uninterrupted octosyllable more than ever; but that verse, if a poet knows how to manage it, is not so unsuited for story-telling as Ellis thought; and Scott had here more story to tell than in any of his preceding pieces, except *Marmion*.

The only character, indeed, in which one takes much interest is Bertram Risingham; but he is a really excellent person, the cream of Scott's ruffians, whether in prose or verse; appearing well, conducting himself better, and ending best of all. Nor is Oswald, the contrasted villain, by any means to be despised; while the passages – on which the romance, in contradistinction to the classical epic, stands or falls – are equal to all but the very best in *Marmion* or the *Lay*. Bertram's account of the first and happier events at Marston Moor, as well as of his feelings as to his comradeship with Mortham; the singularly beautiful opening of the second canto –

'Far in the chambers of the west'

– with the description of Upper Teesdale; Bertram's clamber on the cliff, with its reminiscences of the 'Kittle Nine Steps' – these lead on to many other things that are just as good, ending with that altogether admirable bit of workmanship, Bertram's revenge on Oswald and his own death. Matilda is one of the best of Scott's verse heroines, except Constance – that is to say, the best of his good girls – and she has the interest of being said to have been modelled on 'Green Mantle'. Nor in any of the poems do the lyrics give more satisfactory setting-off to the main text. Indeed, it may be questioned whether any contains such a garland as – to mention only the best – is formed by,

'O, Brignall banks are wild and fair'

and the exquisite,

'A weary lot is thine, fairmaid'

adapted from older matter with a skill worthy of Burns himself; the capital bravura of Allen-a-Dale; and that noble Cavalier lyric,

> 'When the dawn on the mountain was
> misty and grey.'

The Bridal of Triermain was published in 1813, not long after *Rokeby*, and, like that poem, drew its scenery from the North of England; but in circumstances, scale, and other ways it forms a pair with *Harold the Dauntless*, and they had best be noticed together.

The Lord of the Isles, the last of the great quintet, appeared in December 1814. Scott had obtained part of the scenery for it in an earlier visit to the Hebrides, and the rest in his yachting voyage (see below) with the Commissioners of Northern Lights, which also gave the scenic background for *The Pirate*. The poem was not more popular than *Rokeby* in England, and it was even less so in Scotland, chiefly for the reason, only to be mentioned with all but silent amazement, that it was 'not bitter enough against England'. Its faults are, of course, obvious enough. There is simply no central story; the inconvenience that arises to the hero from his being courted by two young ladies cannot awake any very sympathetic tear, nor does either Edith of Lorn or Isabel Bruce awaken any violent desire to offer to relieve him of one of them. The versification, however, is less uniform than that of *Rokeby* or *The Lady of the Lake*, and there are excellent passages – the best being, no doubt, the Abbot's extorted blessing on the Bruce; the great picture of Loch Coruisk, which, whatever people might say, is marvellously faithful; part of the voyage; the landing in Carrick; the rescue of the supposed page; and, finally, Bannockburn, which even Jeffrey admired, though its want of 'animosity' shocked him.

The two last of the great poems – there was indeed a third, *The Field of Waterloo*, written hastily for a subscription, and not worthy either of Scott or of the subject – are by no means the least praiseworthy. Both were issued anonymously, and with indications intended to mislead readers into the idea that they were by Erskine; the intention being, it would seem, partly to ascertain how far the author's mere name counted in his popularity, partly also to test the wind as to the veering of the public taste regarding the verse romance in general.

In both pieces the author fell back upon his earlier scheme of metre, the *Christabel* blend of iambic with anapaestic passages, instead of the nearly pure iambs of his middle poems. The *Bridal*, partly to encourage the idea of Erskine as author, it would seem, is hampered by an intermixed outline-story, told in the introductions, of the wooing and winning of a certain Lucy by a certain Arthur, both of whom may be very heartily wished away. But the actual poem is more thoroughly a Romance of Adventure than even the *Lay*, has much more central interest than that poem, and is adorned by passages of almost as much beauty as can be found in the best of the earlier piece. It is astonishing how anyone with any intelligent knowledge of Scott's work could have entertained the slightest doubt about the authorship of:

> 'Come hither, come hither, Henry my
> page,
> Whom I saved from the sack of Hermit-
> age.'

Let alone that of the well-known opening of the Third Canto, one of the triumphs of that 'science of names' in which Scott was such a proficient:

> 'Bewcastle now must keep the Hold,
> Speir-Adam's steeds must bide in stall,
> Of Hartley-burn the bowmen bold
> Must only shoot from battled wall;
> And Liddesdale may buckle spur,
> And Teviot now may belt the brand,
> Tarras and Ewes keep nightly stir,
> And Eskdale foray Cumberland!'

But these lines are only the most unmistakable, not the best. The opening specification of the Bride; the admirable 'Lyulph's Tale', with the first appearance of the castle, and the stanza (suggested no doubt by a famous picture) of the damsels dragging Arthur's war-gear; the courtship, and Guendolen's wiles to retain Arthur, and the parting; the picture of the King's court; the tournament; all these are good enough. But it is perhaps possible that the description of Sir Roland's tantalized vigil in the Vale of St John, with the moonlit valley, and the sudden and successful revelation of the magic hold when the knight flings his battle-axe, might even surpass the Tale.

Nor are the actual adventures of this Childe Roland in the dark towers inferior. The trials and temptations are of stock material, but all the best matter is stock, and this is handled with a rush and dash which more than saves it. Hopefully the tiger was only a magic tiger, and went home comfortably with the damsels of Zaharak. It seems unfair that he should be actually killed. But this is the only thing that disquiets the reader; and it is impossible to praise too much De Vaux's ingenious compromise between tasteless asceticism and dangerous indulgence in the matter of 'Asia's willing maids'.

Harold the Dauntless is much slighter, as indeed might be expected, considering that it was finished in a hurry, long after the author had given up poetry as a main occupation. But the half burlesque Spenserians of the overture are very good; the contrasted songs, 'Dweller of the Cairn' and 'A Danish Maid for Me', are happy. Harold's interview with the Chapter is a famous bit of bravura; and all concerning the Castle of the Seven Shields, from the ballad introducing it, through the description of its actual appearance (in which, by the way, Scott shows almost a better grasp of the serious Spenserian stanza than anywhere else) to the final battle of Odin and Harold, is of the very best Romantic quality. Perhaps, indeed, it is because (as the *Critical Review*, the Abdiel of 'classical' orthodoxy among the reviews of the time, scornfully said), 'both poems are romantic enough to satisfy all the parlour-boarders of all the ladies' schools in England', that they are so pleasant. It is something, in one's grey and critical age, to feel genuine sympathy with the parlour-boarder.

Despite great felicities of a certain kind, these poems have no claim to formal perfection, and occasionally sin by very great carelessness, if not by something worse. The poet frankly shows himself as one whose appeal is not that of 'jewels five words long', set and arranged in phrases of that magical and unending beauty which the very greatest poets of the world command. His effect, even in description, is rather of mass than of detail. He does not attempt analysis in character, and only skirts

77

passion. Although lavish enough with incident, he is very careless of connected plot. But his great and abiding glory is that he revived the art, lost for centuries in England, of telling an interesting story in verse, of riveting the attention through thousands of lines of poetry neither didactic nor argumentative.

And of his separate passages, his patches of description and incident, when the worst has been said of them, it will remain true that, in their own way and for their own purpose, they cannot be surpassed. The already noticed comparison of any of Scott's best verse-tales with *Christabel*, which they formally imitated to some extent, and with the *White Doe of Rylstone*, which followed them, will no doubt show that Coleridge and Wordsworth had access to mansions in the house of poetry where Scott is never seen. But in some respects even their best passages are not superior to his; and as tales, as romances, his are altogether superior to theirs.

CHAPTER IV

*T*HE NOVELS, FROM *WAVERLEY* TO *REDGAUNTLET*

In the opening introduction to the collected edition of the novels, Scott has given a very full account of the genesis of *Waverley*. These introductions, written before the final inroad had been made on his powers by the united strength of physical and moral misfortune, animated at once by the last glow of those powers, and by the indefinable charm of a fond retrospection, displaying every faculty in autumn luxuriance, are so delightful that they sometimes seem to be the very cream and essence of his literary work in prose. Indeed, it is surprising that they were not published separately as a *History of the Waverley Novels* by their author. Yet the public seems never to have read them very widely. An exception, however, may possibly have been made in the case of this first one, opening as it has long done every new issue of the whole set of novels. At any rate, in one way or another, it is probably known, at least to those who take an interest in Scott, that he had begun *Waverley* and thrown it aside some ten years before its actual appearance, at a time when he was yet a novice in writing literature. He had also attempted one or two other things – a completion of Strutt's *Queenhoo Hall*, the beginning of a tale about Thomas the Rhymer, etc., which are now appended to the introduction itself – and he had once, in 1810, resumed *Waverley*, and again thrown it aside. At last, when his supremacy as a popular poet was threatened by Byron, and when, perhaps, he himself was a little wearying of the verse tale, he discovered the fragment while searching for fishing-tackle in the old desk where he had put it, and after a while made up his mind to make a new and anonymous attempt on public favour.

By the time – 1814 – that the book actually appeared, considerable changes, both for good and for bad, had occurred in Scott's circumstances; and the total of his literary work, independently of the poems mentioned in the last chapter, had been a good deal increased. Ashestiel had been exchanged for Abbotsford; the new house was being planned and carried out so as to become, if not exactly a palace, something much more than the cottage which had been first talked of; and the owner's passion for buying, at extravagant prices, every neighbouring patch of mostly thankless soil that he could get hold of was growing by indulgence. He himself, in 1811 and the following years, was extremely happy and extremely busy, planting trees, planning rooms, working away at *Rokeby* and *Triermain* in the general sitting room of the makeshift house, with hammering all about him (now, the hammer and the pen are perhaps of all manual implements the most deadly and irreconcilable foes!), corresponding with all sorts and conditions of men; furnishing introductions and contributions to all sorts and conditions of books, and struggling, as best he saw his way, though the way was unfortunately not the right one, with the ever-increasing difficulties of Ballantyne & Company. It is quite possible that Dickens consciously took his humorous incarnation of the duties of a 'Co' from Scott's own experience.

But Scott as certainly had to provide the money, the sense, the good-humour, and the rest of the working capital as Mark Tapley himself. The financial part of these matters may be left to the next chapter; it is sufficient to say that, aggravated by misjudgment in the selection and carrying out of the literary part, it brought the firm in 1814 very close to the complete smash which actually happened ten years later. It is tempting to wish that the crash had come, for it was only averted by the alliance with Constable which was the cause of the final downfall. Also, it would have come at a time when Scott was physically better able to bear it; it could hardly in any degree have interfered with the appearance of *Waverley* and its followers; and it would have had at least a chance of awakening their author to a sense of the double mistake of engaging his credit in directly commercial concerns, and of sinking his money in land and building. However, things were to be as they were, and not otherwise.

How anxious Constable must have been to recover Scott (Hunter, the stone of stumbling, was now removed by death) is evident from the mere list of the titles of the books which he took over in whole or part from the Ballantynes. Even his Napoleonic audacity quailed before the *Edinburgh Annual Register*, with its handsome annual loss of a thousand a year, at Brewster's *Persian Astronomy*, in quarto and octavo, and at *General Views of the County of Dumfries*. But he saddled himself with a good deal of the 'stock' (which in this case most certainly had not its old sense of 'assets'), and in May 1813, Scott seems to have thought that if John Ballantyne would curb his taste for long-dated bills, things might go well. Unluckily, John did not choose to do so, and Scott, despite the warning, was equally unable to curb his own for peat bogs, marl-pits, the Cauldshiels Loch, and splendid lots of ancient armour.

By July there was again trouble, and in August things were so bad that they were only rescued by Scott's obtaining from the Duke of Buccleuch a guarantee for £4,000. It was in consenting to this that the Duke expressed his approval of Scott's determination to refuse the Laureateship, which had been offered to him, and which, in consequence of his refusal and at his suggestion, was conferred upon Southey. Even the guarantee, though it did save the firm, saved it with great difficulty.

In the following winter, Scott had an adventure with his eccentric German amanuensis, Henry Weber, who had for some time been going mad, and who proposed a duel with pistols (which he produced) to his employer in the study at Castle Street. *Swift* appeared at last in the summer, and it was in June 1814 that the first of a series of wonderful *tours de force* was achieved by the completion, in about three weeks, of the last half of *Waverley*.

One of the most striking things in Lockhart is the story of the idle apprentice who became industrious by seeing Scott's hand traversing the paper hour after hour at his study window. The novel actually appeared on 7 July, and, being anonymous, made no immediate 'move', as booksellers say, before Scott set off a fortnight later for his long-planned tour with the Commissioners of Northern Lights – the Scottish Trinity House – in their yacht, round the northern half of the island and to Orkney and Shetland. His own account of the tour is well worth the reading for anyone who has an interest in Scotland and in Scott. When he returned in September, Scott was met by two pieces of bad and good tidings respectively – the death of the Duchess of Buccleuch, and the distinct, though not as yet 'furious', success of his novel.

There is no doubt that the early fragments in tale telling which have been mentioned above do not display any particular skill in the art; nor is there much need to quarrel with those who declare that the opening of *Waverley* itself ranks little, if at all, above them. In fact, most people plunge almost at once into the Tullyveolan visit. By doing so, however, they miss not merely the critical pleasure of comparing a man's work (as can rarely be done) during his period of groping for the way, with his actual stumble into it for the first time, but also such justification as there is for the hero's figure. Nobody ever judged the unlucky captain of Gardiner's better than his creator, who at the time frankly called him 'a sneaking piece of imbecility', and declared, with as much probability as right, that 'if he had married Flora, she would have set him up on the chimney-piece, as Count Borowlaski's wife used to do.' But his weaknesses have at least an excuse from his education and antecedents, an excuse that cannot be seen if these antecedents are neglected.

Still, the story-interest only begins when Waverley rides into the bear-warded avenue; it certainly never ceases till the golden image of the same totem is replaced in the Baron of Bradwardine's hand. And it is very particularly to be observed that this interest is of a kind absolutely novel in combination and idiosyncrasy. The elements of literary interest are nowhere new, except in what is, for all we know, accidentally the earliest literature *to us*. They are all to be found in Homer, in the

84

Book of Job, in the *Agamemnon*, in *Lancelot*, in the *Poem of the Cid*. But from time to time, in the hands of the men of greater genius, they are shaken up once more, they are given new adjustments, and a touch of something personal is added which transforms them. This new adjustment and touch produced in Scott's case what we call the Historical Novel.

It is quite a mistake to think that he was limited to this. *Guy Mannering* and *The Antiquary* among the earlier novels, *St Ronan's Well* and the exquisite introductory sketch to the *Chronicles of the Canongate* among the later, would disprove that. But the historical novel was the new kind that he was 'born to introduce', after many failures in many generations. It is difficult to say whether it was accident or property which made his success in it co-existent with his success in depicting national character, scenery, and manners. Attempts at this, not always unsuccessful attempts, had indeed been made before. It had been tried frequently, though usually in the sense of caricature, on the stage; it had been done quite recently in the novel by Miss Edgeworth (whom Scott at least professed to regard as his governess here), and much earlier in this very department of Scotch matters by Smollett. But it had never been done with such commanding ability on such a grand scale.

In *Waverley*, Scott supplied these two aspects, the historical-romantic and the national-characteristic, with a felicity perhaps all the more unerring in that it seems to have been only partly conscious. The subject of 'the Forty-five' was now fully out of taboo, and yet it held an interest that was more than purely historical. The author had vast stores of knowledge at his fingertips, and that sympathy which is so invaluable to the artist when he keeps it within the limits of art. He seems to have possessed by instinct (for there was nobody to teach him) the most important secret of the historical novelist, the secret of making his central and prominent characters fictitious, and the real ones mostly subsidiary.

On the other hand, the knowledge of his native country, which he had been accumulating for almost the whole of his nearly four-and-forty years of life, was combined in him with that universal knowledge of humanity which only men of the greatest genius have. It is certainly true that both these positions have been attacked. One critic made his complaint with the following words: 'Scott only knew a small portion of human nature, and he was unable to portray the physiognomy of the past.' But such criticism is generally considered to be unjustified, and it is the opinion of the majority of readers that Waverley and its successors showed that their author had a real knowledge, complete in all but certain small parts, of human nature, and an almost unlimited faculty of portraying the physiognomy of the past.

The book was published anonymously; very few people knew the real authorship, and few were able to guess at it. It is therefore not surprising that it did not achieve great success immediately. Lockhart says that the slowness of the success was exaggerated, but his own figures prove that it was somewhat leisurely. Five editions, one (the second) of two thousand, the others of one thousand each, supplied the demand of the first six months, and a thousand copies more that of the next eighteen months. This difference from the almost instantaneous myriads of the poems, is quite enough to show very clearly how low the prose novel then stood in popular favour. It is the greatest triumph of Scott that from such a slow start, repeated publications increased the warmth of the book's reception by the public. After a year or two, when the fourth publication was about to come out, Constable actually dared to start with ten thousand copies at once, and they were all absorbed in no time.

Scott had always been a rapid worker, but it was only now, under the combined stimulus of the new-found gift, the desire for more land and a statelier Abbotsford, and the pressure of the affairs of Ballantyne & Co, that he began to work at the furious rate which, although it did not adversely affect the quality of his writing, almost certainly endangered his health. During 1814 he had written nearly all his *Life of Swift*, nearly all *Waverley*, *The Lord of the Isles*, and an abundance of 'small wares';

essays, introductions, and so on. The major part of *Guy Mannering* – perhaps the very best of the novels, for merit of construction and interest of detail – seems to have been written in less than a month, in the final days of this year and the beginning of 1815. The whole appears to have been done in six weeks, to 'shake himself free of *Waverley*' – probably the most gigantic exhibition of the 'hair of the dog' recorded in literature.

The main theme of this novel was furnished by a Dumfries surveyor of taxes, Mr Train, the scenery by that early visit to Galloway, in the interest of the reverend toyer with sweetie-wives, which has been recorded. Other indebtedness, such as that of Hatteraick to the historical or legendary free-trader, Yawkins, and the like, has been traced. But the charm of the whole lies in none of these things, nor in all together, but in Scott's own way of working them up.

Nothing at first could seem to be a greater contrast with *Waverley* than this tale. No big wars, no political hazards; but a double and tenfold portion of human nature and local colour. This last element had in the earlier book been almost entirely supplied by Tullyveolan and its master; for Fergus and the Highland scenes, good as they are, are not much more than a furbishing up of the poem-matter of this kind, especially in the *Lady of the Lake*. But here the supply of character was generous and the variety of scenery extraordinary. We cannot judge the innovation fully now, but let anyone turn to the theatrical properties of Godwin and Holcroft, of Mrs Radcliffe and 'Monk' Lewis, and he will begin to have a better idea of what *Guy Mannering* must have been to its first readers.

As usual, the personages who head the *dramatis personæ* are not the best. Bertram, though less of an idiot than Waverley, is not very much; Lucy is a less lively picture of angelic naiveté than Rose, and nothing else; and Julia's genteel-comedy missishness does not do much more than pair off with Flora's tragedy-queen air. 'Mannering, Guy, a Colonel returned from the Indies', is, perhaps, also too fair a description of the player of the title-part. But the reader does not become so absorbed with the characters of these persons. The real characters are elsewhere. The author opens fire on us almost at the very first with Dominie Sampson and Meg Merrilees, and the equally excellent figure of Bertram's well-meaning booby of a father. Hardly has the reader had time to make their acquaintance when Scott brings on Dandie Dinmont, followed by the almost superfluous reinforcements of Mr Pleydell. In addition to these, he throughout throws in Hatteraick and Glossin, Jock Jabos and his mistress, and Sir Robert Haslewood, the company at Kippletringan, and at the funeral, and elsewhere, in the most reckless spirit of literary lavishness. He is equally generous with incident and scene. The opening passage of Mannering's night-ride could not have been bettered at the cost of any effort on the part of the author. Bertram's walk and the skirmish with the prowlers are simply excellent, and the Edinburgh scenes have always been appreciated and admired as the very best of their kind.

The various passages which lead to the working out of justice on Glossin and Hatteraick are not merely told with a gusto which is ever-present in the author's work, but are also arranged with a craftsmanship which is unfortunately less obvious in some of his later writing. There is hardly any book of Scott's on which it is more tempting to dwell than this. Although the demand had not yet reached anything like its height, two thousand copies were sold in forty-eight hours, and five thousand in three months.

In March 1815, Scott went to London, and here he met with two people of distinction; the Regent and Lord Byron. With Byron, Scott was at once on very good terms, for Scott was not the man to bear any grudge for the early fling in *English Bards and Scotch Reviewers*; and Byron, whatever his faults, 'had more of lion' in him than to be jealous of such a rival. They were quite dissimilar in character, and the difference in their natures was enough to prevent them from being in the strict sense friends. When the two had gone their separate ways, Scott compared Byron to a peacock parted from the hen and lifting up his voice to tell the world about it. The observation was a telling and justified comment on that noble bard's whole life and conversation. But in spite of their differences, there was no animosity or petty jealousy between them, and apparently some real liking.

From London, Scott travelled to Brussels and Paris. The result of this sojourn was, in verse, the already mentioned and not particularly happy *Field of Waterloo*. The outcome in prose was the interesting *Paul's Letters to his Kinsfolk*, an account of the tour. Both were published (the poem almost immediately, *Paul* not till the new year) after Scott's return to Abbotsford at the end of September; and he set to work during the later autumn on his third novel, *The Antiquary*.

The book appeared in May 1816, at about the time of the death of Major John Scott, the last but one of the poet's surviving brothers. It was not at first so popular as *Guy Mannering*, but it very rapidly caught up in this respect: and the bad start is not surprising. To good judges nowadays the book appeals as strongly at least as any other of its author's – in fact, Monkbarns and the Mucklebackits, the rescue of Sir Arthur and Isabel, the scenes in the ruins of St Ruth's, and especially Edie Ochiltree, were never surpassed by him. But the story was a daring innovation, or return, among the novels of its own day. It boldly rejected most of the ordinary sources of romance interest. It had very little plot; its humorous characters, though drawn with the utmost of skill, were not caricatured; and that greatest fault of Scott's – perhaps his only great fault as a novelist – the 'huddling up' of the end, appears in it for the first, though unluckily by no means for the last, time. But it would have been a very sad thing for the public taste if it had definitely refused *The Antiquary*.

A book which contains within the compass of the opening chapters such masterpieces as the journey to the Hawes, the description of the Antiquary's study, and the storm and rescue, must have had a generation of idiots for an audience if it had not been successful. Moreover, it had, as Scott's unwearied biographer has already noted, a new and special source of interest in the admirable fragmentary mottoes, invented to save the greater labour of discovery, which adorn its chapter-headings. Lockhart himself thought that Scott never quite equalled these first three novels. Not everybody would be in agreement with that opinion, but it is none-theless certain that in them Scott discovered, with extraordinary felicity, skill in three different kinds of novel – the historical, the romantic-adventurous, and that of ordinary or almost wholly ordinary life; and that even he never exactly added a fourth kind to his inventions, though he varied them wonder-fully within themselves. The romance partly histori-cal, the romance mainly or wholly fictitious, and the novel of manners; these were his three classes, and hardly any others.

It is not entirely clear what were the reasons which made Scott decide to make his next venture, the *Tales of my Landlord*, under a fresh pseudonym – Jedediah Cleishbotham, and also to publish it not with Constable, but with Murray and Blackwood. Lockhart's blame of John Ballantyne may not be unfair; but it is rather less supported by documentary evidence than most of his strictures on the Ballantynes.

The most likely explanation is to be found in Scott's double dislike, both as an independent person and a man of business, of giving a monopoly of his work to one publisher, and by his constant fancy for trying experiments on the public – a fancy itself not wholly, though partially, understandable. As a matter of fact, *Old Mortality* and *The Black Dwarf* were offered to and pretty eagerly accepted by Murray and Blackwood, on the terms of half profits and the inevitable batch of 'old stock'. The story of the unlucky quarrel with Blackwood in consequence of some critical remarks of his on the end of *The Black Dwarf* – remarks certainly not inexcusable – and of Scott's famous letter in reply, is told with fair detail in the second edition of Lockhart, from the actual archives.

Scott doubled his work during the summer and autumn by undertaking the historical department, relinquished by Southey, of the *Edinburgh Annual Register*, yet the two *Tales* were ready in November, and appeared on the 1 December 1816. Murray wrote effusively to Scott (who, it must be remembered, was not even to his publishers the known author), and received a very amusing reply, from which one sentence may be quoted as an example of those which have brought upon Sir Walter the reproach of falsehood, or at least disingenuousness, from Goodman Dull. 'I assure you,' he writes, 'I have never read a volume of them till they were printed.' A delightful choice of words, for it looks decisive, and means absolutely nothing. Nobody but a magician, and no ordinary magician, could read a *volume* (which in the usual parlance means a printed volume) before it was printed.

To back his disclaimer, Scott offered to review himself in the *Quarterly*, which he did. No one should approve of authors being their own reviewers; though when (as sometimes happens) they have any brains, they probably know the faults and merits of their books better than anyone else, and can at any rate state, with a precision which is too rare in the ordinary critic, what the book is meant to be and tries to do. But this case was clearly an exceptional one, and rather part of an elaborate practical joke than anything else.

Dulness, however, had in many ways found stumbling-blocks in the first foster-children of the excellent Jedediah

Cleishbotham. The very pious and learned, if not exactly humorous or shrewd, Dr McCrie, fell foul of the picture of the Covenanters given in *Old Mortality*. No one who knows the documents is likely to agree with him now, and from hardly any point of view but his could the greatness of the book be denied. Although Scott's humour is by no means absent from it, that quality does not perhaps find quite such an opportunity, even in Mause and Cuddie, as in the Baron, and the Dominie and the inhabitants of Monkbarns.

But as a historical novel, it is a far greater one than *Waverley*. Drumclog, the siege of Tillietudlem, above all, the matchless scene where Morton is just saved from murder by his own party, surpass anything in the earlier book. But greater than any of these single things is one of the first and the greatest of Scott's splendid gallery of romantic historic portraits, the stately figure of Claverhouse. All the features which he himself was to sum up in that undying sentence of 'Wandering Willie's Tale' later are here put in detail and justified.

As for the companion to this masterly book, the earlier part of *The Black Dwarf* is as enjoyable as all but the best of Scott's work. But the character of the *Dwarf* himself was not one that he could manage. The nullity of Earnscliff and Isabel is complete. Isabel's father is a stagy villain, or rather rascal (for Victor Hugo's antithesis between *scélérat* and *maroufle* comes in here), and even Scott has never hustled off a conclusion with such complete lack of care as to anything like completeness. Willie of Westburnflat here, like Christie of the Clinthill later, is one of our old friends of the poems back again, and welcome back again. But he and Hobbie can hardly save a book which Scott seems to have thrown in with its admirable companion, not as a make weight, but rather as a foil.

Between the first and the second sets of *Tales*, the 'author of *Waverley*', true to his odd design of throwing the public off the scent, reappeared, and the result was *Rob Roy*. While he was writing this book, Scott suffered his first attacks of 'cramp of the stomach', which although perhaps unconnected with his later, ultimately fatal illness, no doubt led up to it and gave warning of serious problems to come. Perhaps because of his illness, Scott did not at first much like *Rob*. But he was reconciled later; and hardly anybody else (except those who have never liked his work at all) can ever have had any doubt about it. The end is even more than usually huddled, and the beginning may perhaps have dawdled a little over commercial details (in the opinion of Lady Louisa Stuart). Moreover, the fact that the distribution of time, which lingers over weeks and months before and after it devotes almost the major part of the book to the events of forty-eight hours, is irregular, cannot be denied. But almost from the introduction of Frank to Diana, certainly from his setting off in the grey of the morning with Andrew Fairservice, to the point at least where the heroine stoops from her pony in a manner equally obliging and graceful, there is no dropped stitch, no false note.

Nor in any book are there so many of Scott's own characters, and others not quite so much his own. Helen Macgregor, perhaps, does not 'thrill our blood and over-power our reason', as she did Lady Louisa's, simply because we were so many years later than that acute and accomplished granddaughter of Lady Mary. Rashleigh pretty frequently, Rob himself now and then, may also seem a little too theatrical. But, as a rule, Rob does not; and for nobody else, not even for the fortunate Frank – who has nothing to do but to walk through his part creditably, and does it – need any allowance be made. The Bailie is, with Shallow, his brother justice (upon whom he justly looks down, but to whom he can be said to be kind) in Arthur's bosom; Andrew Fairservice and the Dougal creature, Justice Inglewood and Sir Hildebrand, are there too. As for Di Vernon, she is the one of Scott's heroines with whom one *has to* fall in love, just as, according to a beautiful story, a thoughtless and reluctant world *had to* believe the Athanasian Creed. Some readers – mostly women, have seen her as slightly vulgar. All men, who are men and gentlemen, must

97

delight in her. And here, as always, to all but the very last, even in the twilight of *Anne of Geierstein*, the succession of scenes hurries the reader along without breath or time to stop and criticize, with nothing to do, if he is a reasonable person, but to read and enjoy and admire.

Lockhart has taken the opportunity of this point of time (1817–18), which may be said to mark the zenith of Scott's prosperity, if not of his fame, to halt and to give a sort of survey of his father-in-law's private life at Castle Street and at Abbotsford. It forms one of the pleasantest portions of his book, containing nothing more tragic than the advent of the famous American tragedy of *The Cherokee Lovers*. Its careful author sent it to Scott, in order that he might approve it and publish it, in duplicate. Upon receipt of the two copies, Scott had to pay five pounds twice over for the postage of the rubbish.

During the early part of the same year, the Regalia of Scotland were rediscovered at Edinburgh Castle, a triumph in which Scott played a leading role and an event which underlined the author's singular pride in his homeland and her history.

Naturally, things were not as easy as they seemed. The stomach cramps with which Scott had been already seized, during the progress of *Rob Roy*, continued. Although they were probably not caused by overwork, they were undoubtedly exacerbated by the pace of his writing, and the ferocious manner in which he worked his brains. He had his distractions; friends and acquaintances, long walks and social engagements. But it must be doubted whether social intercourse, or even bodily exercise in company with others, is really the best refreshment after very severe mental labour. They do not refresh, relax, relieve, like a bath of pure solitude.

Various events of importance happened to Scott, in the later course of the year 1818 (besides a much worse recurrence of his disorder), after *The Heart of Midlothian* (the second series of the *Tales*) had been published in June, and *The Bride of Lammermoor* (the third series) had been begun. The Duke of Buccleuch, his chief, his (as he would himself have cheerfully admitted) patron, his helper in time of need, and his most intimate friend, died. So did his brother-in-law, Charles Carpenter. Charles's death added considerably, though to an extent exaggerated at first and only reversionary, to the prospects of Scott's children. Scott gave up an idea, which he had for some time held, of obtaining a judgeship of the Scotch Exchequer; but he received his baronetcy in April 1820. Abbotsford went on gradually and expensively completing itself; the correspondence which tells us so much and is such delightful reading continued, as if the writer had nothing else to write and nothing else to do. But for us the chief matters of interest are the two novels mentioned, and that admirable supplement to the second of them, *The Legend of Montrose*.

There can be little doubt that in at least some passages, and those very large ones, of *The Heart of Midlothian*, Scott went as high as he ever had done, or ever did thereafter. Although, according to Lady Louisa Stuart, 'Mr Saddletree is not amusing', and there is too much Scots law for some English readers, this is not an opinion shared by the majority of people acquainted with the work.

It must be remembered that until Scott opened people's eyes, there were some very particular conventions and prejudices, even in the most receptive of minds, about novels. Technical details were voted tedious and out of place – an opinion that has been partly justified by some of the work of M. Zola and others in years since. Professional matters, the lower middle classes, etc., were thought 'low', as Goldsmith's audience had had it, 'vulgar', as Madame de Stael said of Miss Austen. That the farrago of the novelist's book is absolutely universal and indiscriminate, provided only that he knows what to do with it, had not dawned on the general mind.

On the other hand, Lady Louisa was right in objecting to the finale – it has been admitted that Scott was never good at a conclusion – and George Staunton is rather uninteresting throughout. But how much does this leave! The description of the lynching of Porteous and the matchless interview with Queen Caroline are only the very best of such a series of good things that, except just at the end, it may be said to be uninterrupted. Jeanie it is unnecessary to praise; the same Lady Louisa's admiration of the wonderful art which could attract so much interest to a plain, good, not clever, almost middle-aged woman sums up all. But almost everyone plays up to Jeanie in perfection – her father and, to no small extent, her sister, her husband and Dumbiedykes, Madge Wildfire (a most difficult and most successful character) and her old fiend of mother, the Duke and the tobacco-shop keeper. Abundant as are the good things afterwards, it is probably true to say that Scott never showed his actual original genius, his faculty of creation and combination, to such an extent and in such proportion again.

He certainly did not, according to some critics, in *The Bride of Lammermoor*, a book which, putting the mere fragment of *The Black Dwarf* aside, seems to them like his first approach to failure in prose. Lockhart, whose general critical opinions deserve the profoundest respect, thought differently – thought it, indeed, 'the most pure and perfect of all the tragedies that Scott ever penned'. Perhaps there is something in this of the same ingenuity which Scott himself showed in his disclaimer to Murray quoted above, for tragedy *per se* was certainly not Scott's forte to the same extent as were comedy and history. But it is true that there are many who agree with Lockhart.

On the other hand, it must be said that while we do not know enough of the House of Ravenswood to feel much sympathy with its fortunes as a house, the 'conditions', in the old sense, of its last representative are not such as to attract us much to him personally. He is already far too much of that hero of opera which he was destined to become, a sulky, stagy creature, in theatrical poses and a black-plumed hat, who cannot even play the easy and perennially attractive part of *desdichado* so as to keep our compassion. Lucy is a simpleton so utter and complete that it is difficult even to be sorry for her, especially as Ravenswood would have made a detestable husband. The mother is meant to be and is a repulsive virago, and the father a time-serving and almost vulgar intriguer.

Moreover – and all this is not in the least surprising, since he was in agonies during most of the composition, and nearly died before its close from a violent series of attacks of cramp in the spring of 1819, attacks which he himself believed would prove fatal – the author has, contrary to his usual habits, provided very few subsidiary characters to support or carry off the principals. Caleb Balderstone has been perhaps unfairly objected to by the very persons who praise the whole book;

102

but he is certainly something of a burden. Bucklaw, though agreeable, is very slight; Craigengelt is merely superfluous; the Marquis shadowy. Even such fine things as the hags at the laying-out, and the visit of Lucy and her father to Wolf's Crag, and such amusing ones as Balderstone's *fabliau*-like expedients to raise the wind in the matter of food, hardly save the situation; and though the tragedy of the end is complete, it is in danger of leaving the reader rather cold. One is sorry for Lucy, but it was really her own fault – a Scottish maiden is not usually unaware of the possibilities and advantages of 'kilting her coats of green satin' and flying from the lad she does not love to the lad she does. The total disappearance of Edgar is the best thing that could happen to him, and the only really satisfactory point is Bucklaw's very gentlemanlike sentence of arrest on all impertinent questioners.

But if the companion of the first set of *Tales* was a dead-weight rather than a make-weight, the make-weight of the third would have atoned for anything. It may be said, allowing for scale and conditions, that Scott never did anything much better than *A Legend of Montrose*. First, it is pervaded by the magnificent figure of Dugald Dalgetty. Secondly, the story, though with something of the usual huddle at the end, is interesting throughout, with the minor figures skilfully sketched in. Menteith, though merely outlined, is a good fellow, a gentleman, and not a stick; Allan escapes the merely melodramatic; 'Gillespie Grumach' is masterly in his brief appearances; and Montrose himself is brought in with a skill which has too often escaped notice. For it would mar the story to deal with the tragedy of his end, and his earlier history is a little awkward to manage.

Moreover, that faculty of hurrying on the successive *tableaux* which is so conspicuous in most of Scott's work, and so conspicuously absent in the *Bride* (where there are long passages with no action at all) is eminently present here. The meeting with Dalgetty; the night at Darnlinvarach, from the bravado of the candlesticks to Menteith's tale; the gathering and council of the clans; the journey of Dalgetty, with its central point in the Inveraray dungeon; the escape; and the battle of Inverlochy – these form an exemplary specimen of the kind of interest which Scott's best novels possess as nothing of the kind had before possessed it, and as few things out of Dumas have possessed it since. Nor can the most fervent admirer of Chicot and of Porthos say in cool blood that their creator could have created Dalgetty, who is at once an admirable human being, a wonderful national type of the more eccentric kind, and the embodiment of an astonishing amount of judiciously adjusted erudition.

Many incidents of interest and some of importance

occurred in Scott's private life between the date of 1818 and that of 1820, besides those mentioned already. One of these was the acquisition by Constable of the whole of his back-copyrights for the very large sum of twelve thousand pounds, a contract supplemented twice later in 1821 and 1823 by fresh purchases of rights as they accrued for nominal sums of eleven thousand pounds in addition. Unfortunately, this transaction, like almost all his later ones, was more fictitious than real. And though it was lucky that the publisher never discharged the full debt, so that when his bankruptcy occurred something was saved out of the wreck which would otherwise have been pure loss, the proceeding is characteristic of the mischievously unreal system of money transactions which brought Scott to ruin.

Except for small things like review articles, etc., and for his official salaries, he hardy ever touched real money for the fifteen most prosperous years of his life, between 1810 and 1825. Promises to receive were interchanged with promises to pay in such a bewildering fashion that unless he had kept a chartered accountant of rather unusual skill and industry perpetually at work, it must have been utterly impossible for him to know at any given time what he had, what he owed, what was due to him, and what his actual income and expenditure were. The commonly accepted estimate is that during the most flourishing time, 1820–1825, he made about fifteen thousand a year, and on paper he probably did. Nor can he ever have spent, in the proper sense of the term, anything like that sum, for the Castle Street house cannot have cost, even with lavish hospitality, much to keep up, and the Abbotsford establishment, though liberal, was never ostentatious.

But when large lump sums are constantly expended in purchases of land, building, furnishing, and the like; when every penny of income except official salaries goes through a complicated process of abatement in the way of discounts for six and twelve months' bills, fines for renewal, payments to banks for advances and the like – the 'clean' sums available at any given moment bear quite fantastic and untrustworthy relations to their nominal representatives. It may be strongly suspected, from the admitted decrease of a very valuable practice under Walter Scott senior, and from its practical disappearance under Thomas, that the genius of the Scott family did not precisely lie in the management of money.

The marriage of Sophia, Scott's daughter, to Lockhart, and the purchase of a commission for her eldest brother Walter in the Eighteenth Hussars, made gaps in Scott's family circle, and also, beyond all doubt, in his finances. The first was altogether happy for him. It did not, for at any rate some years, absolutely sever him from the dearest of his children, a lady who, to judge from her portraits, must have been of singular charm, and who seems to have been the only one of the four with much of his mental characteristics. Moreover, in Lockhart he found an agreeable companion, a loyal friend, and an incomparable biographer.

Of his son, Sir Walter Scott the second and last, not much personal detail is obtainable. The few anecdotes handed down, and his father's letters to him (we have no replies), suggest a good sort of person, slightly foolish and over-eager in the wrong places, with next to no intellectual gifts, and perhaps more his mother's son than his father's. He had some difficulties in his first regiment, which seems to have been a wild one, and not in the best form; he married an heiress of the unpoetical name of Jobson, to whom and of whom his father writes with a pretty old-fashioned affection and courtesy, which perhaps gave Thackeray some traits for Colonel Newcome. Of the younger brother Charles, an Oxford man, who went into the Foreign Office, there is even less record than of Walter. Anne Scott, the third of the family, and the faithful attendant of her father in the terrible days of his final illness, died in her sister's house shortly after Sir Walter, and Mrs Lockhart herself followed before the *Life* was finished. Scott can hardly be said to have bequeathed good luck to any of these his descendants.

It was at the end of 1819, after Walter the younger left home, and before Sophia's marriage, that the next in order of the *Waverley Novels* (now again such by title, and not *Tales of my Landlord*) appeared. This was *Ivanhoe*, which was published in a rather costlier shape than its forerunners, and yet sold to the extent of twelve thousand copies in its three-volume form. Lockhart, perhaps with one of the few but graceful escapes of national predilection (it ought not to be called prejudice) to be noticed in him, pronounces this a greater work of art, but a lesser in genius than its purely Scottish predecessors. As there is nothing specially English in *Ivanhoe*, but only an attempt to delineate Normans and Saxons before the final blend was formed, an Englishman may, perhaps, claim at least impartiality if he accepts the positive part of Lockhart's judgment and disagrees with the negative.

Although the worst of Scott's cramps were past, he was still in anything but good health when he composed the novel, most of which was dictated, not written; and his avocations and bodily troubles together may have had something to do with those certainly pretty flagrant anachronisms which have brought on *Ivanhoe* the wrath of Dryasdust. But Dryasdust is *adeo negligibile ut negligibilius nihil esse possit*, and the book is a great one from beginning to end. The mere historians who quarrel with it have probably never read the romances which justify it, even from the point of view of literary 'document'.

The picturesque opening; the Shakespearean character of Wamba; the splendid Passage of Arms; the more splendid siege of Torquilstone; the gathering up of a dozen popular stories of the 'King-and-the-Tanner' kind into the episodes of the Black Knight and the Friar; the admirable, if a little conventional, sketch of Bois-Guilbert, the pendant in prose to Marmion; the more admirable contrast of Rebecca and Rowena; and the final Judgment of God, which for once vindicates Scott from the charge of never being able to wind up a novel – with such subsidiary sketches as Gurth, Prior Aymer, Isaac, Front-de-Boeuf, Athelstane, and others – give such an abundance of creative and descriptive wealth as nobody but Scott has ever put together in prose. Even the nominal hero, it will be noticed, escapes the curse of most of Scott's young men (the young men to several of whom Thackeray would have liked to be mother-in-law), and if he is not worthy of Rebecca, he does not get her. As for Richard, no doubt, he is not the Richard of history, but what does that matter? He is a most admirable recreation, softened and refined, of the Richard of a romance which, be it remembered, is itself in all probability as old as the thirteenth century.

After speaking frankly of *The Bride of Lammermoor* and of some others of Scott's works, it may perhaps be permissible to rate the successor to *Ivanhoe* rather higher than it was rated at the time, or than it has generally been rated since. When it was published in March 1820, *The Monastery* was regarded as a failure; it is said that a sincere admirer of Scott once confided to a fellow admirer the opinion that 'a good deal of it really is rot, you know.' But this is not entirely true. Undoubtedly it does not rank with the very best, or even next to them. In returning to Scottish ground, Scott may have strengthened himself on one side, but from the distance of the times and the obscure and comparatively uninteresting period which he selected (just after the strange and rapid panorama of the five Jameses and before the advent of Queen Mary), he lost as much as he gained. An intention, afterwards abandoned, to make yet another fresh start, and try a new double on the public by appearing neither as 'Author of *Waverley*' nor as Jedediah Cleishbotham, may have hampered him a little, though it gave a pleasant introduction. The supernatural part, though much better than is generally admitted, is no doubt not entirely satisfactory, being uncertainly handled, and subject to the warning of *Nec deus infersit*. There is some return of that super-abundance of internal and inaction which has been noted in *The Bride*.

And, above all, there appears here a fault which had not been noticeable before, but which was to increase in Scott's writing – the fault of introducing a character as if he were to be of great pith and moment, and then letting his interest simply tail off. The trouble taken about Halbert by personages natural and supernatural promises the case of some extraordinary figure, and he is but very ordinary. Still, would the work of any other authors except Scott be so criticized, if in spite of all this, they gave us anything like the wonderful descriptions of Glendearg, the scenes in the Abbey, the night-ride of poor Father Philip, the escape from the Castle of Avenel, the passage of the interview of Halbert with Murray and Morton? Even the episode of Sir Piercie Shafton, though it cannot be argued that Scott has by any means truly represented Euphuism, is good and amusing in itself; while there are those who boldly like the White Lady personally. She is more futile than a sprite seems; but she is distinctly 'nice'.

At any rate, nobody could (or indeed did) deny that the author, six months later, made up for any shortcoming in *The Abbot*, where, except in the end (eminently of the huddled order), everything is as it should be. The heroine is, with the exception of Di Vernon, Scott's masterpiece in that kind, while all the Queen Mary scenes are unsurpassed in his work, and rarely equalled in the work of any other author. Nor was there any falling off in *Kenilworth* (January 1821), where he again shifted his scene to England. He has not indeed interested us very much personally in Amy Robsart, but as an unlucky heroine she is in every way superior to Lucy Ashton. Of all Scott's books, this one was the 'novel without a hero', and, considering his defects in that direction, this was hardly a drawback. In fact, it cannot be said to have any one minor character which stands out as having particular merit. But the whole work is interesting throughout. The journeys of Tressilian to Devonshire and of Amy and Wayland to Kenilworth have the curious attraction which Scott, a great traveller, and a lover of it, knew how to give to journeys, and the pageantry and Court scenes, at Greenwich and elsewhere, command the respect and admiration of the reader. Indeed, *Kenilworth* is equal in standard to any of the novels in sustained variety of interest, and, unlike too many of them, it comes to a real end.

It was in 1821 that a book now necessarily much forgotten and even rare, Adolphus's *Letters on the Author of Waverley*, at once showed the interest taken in the identity of the 'Great Unknown', and fixed it as being that of the author of the *Lay*, with a great deal of ingenuity and with a most industrious abundance of arguments, bad and good. After such a proof of public interest, it is hardly surprising that both Scott and Constable renewed their efforts, working what has been shamefully called the 'novel manufactory' at the highest pressure. *The Pirate, The Fortunes of Nigel, Peveril of the Peak, Quentin Durward, St Ronan's Well,* and *Redgauntlet* were written and published in very rapid succession. These books, almost all of wonderful individual excellence (*Peveril* being, perhaps the only exception to this rule), and of still more wonderful variety, were succeeded, before the crash of 1825–26, by the *Tales of the Crusaders*, commendable in part, if not as a whole. When we think that all these were, with some other work, accomplished in less than five years, it seems reasonable rather than presumptuous on the part of the author and well-judged rather than rash on the part of the bookseller, to agree upon a contract for four of them in a batch – a batch unnamed, unplanned, not even yet in embryo, but simply existing *in potentia* in the brain of Walter Scott himself.

In the consideration of this batch as a whole, written when the first novelty of the novels was long over, and before there was any decline in quality, it is possible to get from these books, as well as from any other division of his works, an idea of their author's miraculous power. Many novelists since have written as much or more in the same time. But their books for the most part, even when well above the average, popular, and deservedly popular too, leave next to no trace on the mind. You do not want to read them again; you remember, even with a strong memory, nothing special about their plots; above all, their characters take little or no hold on the mind in the sense of becoming part of its intellectual circle and range.

How different is it with these six or eight novels, 'written with as much care as the others, that is to say, with none at all,' as the author wickedly remarked! *The Pirate* (December 1821) leads off, its scenery rendered with the faithfulness of recent memory, and yet adjusted and toned by the seven years' interval since Scott yachted round Orkney and Shetland. Here are the admirable characters of Brenda (slight yet thoroughly pleasing), and her father, the not too melodramatic ones of Minna, Cleveland, and Norna, the triumph of Claud Halcro (to whom few do justice), and again, the excellent keeping of story and scenery to character and incident.

The Fortunes of Nigel (May 1822) originated in a proposed series of 'Letters of the Seventeenth Century', in which others were to take part, and perhaps marks a certain decline, though only in senses to be distinctly defined and limited. Nothing that Scott ever did is better than the portrait of King James, which, in the absence of one from the hand of His Majesty's actual subject for some dozen years, Mr William Shakespeare of New Place, Stratford, is probably the most perfect thing of the kind that ever could have been or can be done. And the picture of Whitefriars, though it is borrowed to a great extent, and rather anticipated in point of time, from Shadwell's *Squire of Alsatia*, sixty or seventy years after date, is of the finest, whilst Sir Mungo Malagrowther all but deserves the same description. But this most can-tankerous knight is not touched off with the complete-ness of Dalgetty, or even of Claud Halcro. Lord Glenvarloch adds, to the insipidity which is the bane of Scott's good heroes, some rather disagreeable traits which none of them had previously shown. Dalgarno in the same way falls short of his best bad heroes. Dame Suddlechop suggests, for the first time unfavourably, a Shakespearean ancestress, Mistress Quickly, and the story halts and fails to carry the reader rapidly over the stony path. Even Richie Moniplies, even Gentle Geordie, good as both are, fall short of their predecessors.

Ten years earlier *The Fortunes of Nigel* would have been a miracle, and one might have said, 'If a man begins like this, what will he do later?' Now, thankless and often uncritical as is the chatter about 'writing out', we can hardly compare *Nigel* with *Guy Mannering*, or *Rob Roy*, or even *The Abbot*, and not be conscious of something that (to use a favourite quotation of Scott's own), 'doth appropinque an end', though an end as yet far distant. The 'bottom of the sack', as the French say, is still a long way off; but it is within measurable distance.

Even a friendly critic must admit that this distance seemed to be alarmingly shortened by *Peveril of the Peak* (January 1823), which among the full-sized novels is arguably his least good book, worse even than 'dotages', as they are sometimes thought, like *Anne of Geierstein* and *Count Robert*. No one has defended the story, which, languid as it is, is made worse by the long gaps between the passages that ought to be interesting, and by a (for Scott) quite abnormal and portentous absence of really characteristic characters. Lockhart argues a case for some of these, but his pleas can hardly be admitted. It is likely that those who read Scott pretty regularly are always sorely tempted to skip *Peveril* altogether, and that when they do read it, they find the chariot wheels drive with a heaviness of which elsewhere they are entirely unconscious.

But in the same year (1823), *Quentin Durward* not only made up for *Peveril*, but showed Scott's powers to be at least as great as when he wrote *The Abbot*, if not as great as ever. He has taken some liberties with history, but no more than he was perfectly entitled to take; he has paid the historic muse with ample interest for anything she lent him, by the magnificent sketch of Louis and the fine one of Charles; he has given a more than passable hero in Quentin, and a very agreeable if not ravishing heroine in Isabelle. Above all, he has victoriously shown his old faculty of conducting the story with such a series of enthralling, even if sometimes episodic passages, that nobody but a pedant of 'construction' would take the pains to enquire in any detail whether they actually make a whole. Quentin's meeting with the King and his rescue from Tristan by the archers; the interviews between Louis and Crevecceur, and Louis and the Astrologer; the journey (another of Scott's admirable journeys); the sack of Schonwaldt, and the feast of the Boar of Ardennes; Louis in the lion's den at Peronne – these are things that are simply of the first order. Nor need the conclusion, which has shocked some, shock any who do not hold, with critics of the Rymer school, that 'the hero ought always to be successful.' For as Quentin wins Isabelle at last, what more success need we want? And why should not Le Balafré, that loyal Leslie, be the instrument of his nephew's good fortune?

The recovery was perfectly well maintained in *St Ronan's Well* (still 1823) and *Redgauntlet* (1824), the last novels of full length before the downfall. They were also, it must be noticed, the first planned (while *Quentin* itself was completed) after Scott suffered some early symptoms of apoplectic seizure, or stroke, which might, even if they had not been helped by one of the severest turns of fortune that any man ever experienced, have served as punishment Scott's daring contempt of ordinary laws in the working of his brains. The harm done to *St Ronan's Well* by the author's giving in to James Ballantyne's Philistine prudery in protesting against the original story (in which Clara did not discover the cheat put on her till a later period than the ceremony) is generally acknowledged. As it is, not merely is the whole thing made

117

a much ado about nothing – for no law and no Church in Christendom would have hesitated to declare the nullity of a marriage which had never been consummated, and which was celebrated while one of the parties took the other for someone else – but Clara's shattered reason, Tyrrel's despair, and Etherington's certainty that he has the cards in his hand, are all incredible and unaccountable – mere mid-winter madness. Nevertheless, this, Scott's only attempt at actual contemporary fiction, has extraordinary interest and great merit as such, while Meg Dods would save half a dozen novels, and the society at the Well is hardly inferior.

And then came *Redgauntlet*. A great lover of Scott once nearly invoked the assistance of Captain McTurk to settle matters with a friend of his who would not pronounce *Redgauntlet* the best of all the novels, and would only go so far as to admit that it contains some, and many, of the best things. The best as a novel it cannot be called, because the action is desultory in the extreme. There are wide gaps even in the chain of story interest that does exist, and the conclusion, while in itself worthy of praise, is even for Scott, too disconnected with the concern of the principal characters. But even putting 'Wandering Willie's Tale' aside, and taking for granted the merits of that incomparable piece, the good things in this fascinating book defy exaggeration. The unique autobiographic interest – so fresh and keen and personal, and yet so free from the odious intrusion of actual personality – of the earlier epistolary presentation of Saunders and Alan Fairford, of Darsie and Green Mantle; Peter Peebles, equal to Scott's best; Alan's journey and Darsie's own wanderings; the scenes at the Provost's dinner-table and in Tam Turnpenny's den; that unique figure, the skipper of the *Jumping Jenny*; the extraordinarily effective presentation of Prince Charles, already in his decadence, if not yet in his dotage; the profusion of smaller sketches and vignettes everywhere grouped round the mighty central triumph of the adventures of Piper Steenie – who but Scott has done such things? He never put so much again in a single book.

There is something in it which it is hardly fanciful to take as a 'note of finishing', as the last piece of the work, that, gigantic as it was, was not exactly collar work, not sheer hewing of wood and drawing of water for the taskmasters. And it was fitting that the book, so varied, so fresh, so gracious and kindly, so magnificent in part, with a magnificence dominating Scott's usual range, should begin with the beginnings of his own career, and should end with the practical finish, not merely of the good days, but of the days that dawned with any faint promise of goodness, in the career of the last hope of the Jacobite cause.

CHAPTER

V

THE DOWNFALL OF BALLANTYNE & COMPANY

Redgauntlet, it has been said, was the last novel on the full scale before the downfall of Scott's prosperity. But before this he had begun *The Life of Napoleon* and *Woodstock*, and, in June 1825, had published the *Tales of the Crusaders*, which contain some work almost, if not quite, equal to his best, and which rose at first to a greater popularity than their immediate predecessors. It was, and generally is, held that *The Betrothed*, the earlier of the two, was saved by *The Talisman*; and there can be no doubt that the latter is the better. Contrary to the habit of novelists, Scott was at least as happy with Richard here as he had been in *Ivanhoe*, and though he owed a good deal in both to the presentation of his hero in the very interesting romance published by his old secretary Weber – one of the best of all the English verse romances and the first English poem to show a really English patriotism – he owed nothing but suggestion. The duel at the Diamond in the Desert is admittedly one of the most pleasing things of the kind by a master in that kind, and if the adventures in the chapel of Engedi are both a little farcical and a little 'apropos of nothing in particular', the story nowhere else halts or fails till it reaches its real 'curtain' with the second *Accipe hoc!* If it had been longer, it might not have been so strong, but as it is, it is nearly perfect.

But there is also more good in *The Betrothed* than most people will admit. The beginning, the siege of the Garde Doloureuse, and the ghostly adventure of Eveline at the Saxon manor are excellent; while, even later, Scott has entangled the evidence against Damian and the heroine with much of the same skill which he had shown in compromising Waverley. Had not James Ballantyne dashed the author's spirits with some of his petty objections, the whole might have reached the same uniformly high standard as *The Talisman*. Indeed, it must be confessed that, though Lockhart is generous enough on this point to the man to whom he has been accused of being unjust, we have very little evidence of any improvement in Scott's work due to James, and we know that he did harm on more than one occasion. But, as it stands, the book no doubt exhibits the usual faults, that languishing of the middle action, for instance, which injures *The Bride of Lammermoor* and *The Monastery*, together with the much more common huddling and improbability of the conclusion. But it is common knowledge that the conclusion was put on hurriedly, against the author's inclinations, and after he, disgusted by the grumblings of others, had relinquished his work; so its failings are hardly surprising.

It is impossible here to describe in any detail Scott's domestic life during the years which passed since it was last mentioned, years in which he was at his most prosperous and popular. The estate of Abbotsford gradually grew, with large sums of money being paid towards its growth, till the catastrophe itself finally prevented an expenditure of £40,000 in a lump on more land. The house grew likewise, extending to one hundred and fifty feet of front, its exterior displaying a slightly confused but not disagreeable muddle of styles, and reproductions, and incorporated fragments, its interior a blend of museum and seignorial hall. It was practically completed and splendidly 'house-warmed' to celebrate the marriage, on 3 February 1825, of the heir, on whom both house and estate were settled, with, as things turned out, no very fortunate result.

The family continued to divide their time between Abbotsford and Castle Street as usual, when summer and winter, term and vacation, called them. At Abbotsford open house was always kept to a Noah's ark-full of visitors, invited and uninvited, high and low, and Castle Street saw more modest but equally cordial and constant hospitalities. The Lockharts in particular were frequent visitors. Meanwhile, the country home at Chiefswood was a sort of escaping place for Sir Walter when visitors made Abbotsford unbearable. The annual 'Abbotsford Hunt' was greatly enjoyed by the neighbours; and though, as his health grew weaker, Scott found himself less able to take part in athletic exercise or sport and was forced to curtail his activities in those spheres, he still did as much as he was able to manage. In 1822, the great visit of George IV to Scotland took place, and Sir Walter played a major part in all the proceedings; and of this Lockhart has left one of his liveliest and most pleasantly subacid accounts.

Scott made frequent visits to England during this period in his life; and at last, in the summer of 1825, he made a journey, which was a kind of triumphal progress, to Ireland, with his daughter Anne and Lockhart as companions. The party returned by way of the Lakes, and the triumph was, as it were, formally wound up at Windermere in a regatta, with Wilson for admiral of the lake and Canning for joint occupant of the triumphal boat. 'It was roses, roses all the way', till in the autumn of the year the rue began, according to its custom, to take their place.

The immediate cause of the disaster was Scott's secret partnership in the house of Ballantyne & Co, which, dragged down by the greater concerns of Constable & Co in Edinburgh and Hurst, Robinson, & Co in London, failed for the nominal amount of £117,000 at the end of January 1826. Their assets were, in the first place, claims on the two other firms, which realized a mere trifle; and, in the second place, the property, the genius, the life, and the honour of Sir Walter Scott.

When one has to deal briefly with very complicated and much-debated matters, it is most important to confine the dealing to as few points as possible. In this particular case, the number may be limited to two – the nature and amount of the indebtedness itself, and the manner in which it was met. The former, except so far as the total figures on the debtor side are concerned, is the question most in dispute. That the printing business of Ballantyne & Co (the publishing business had lost heavily, but it had long ceased to be a drain), in the ordinary literal sense owed £117,000 – that is to say, that it had lost that sum in business, or that the partners had overdrawn to that amount – nobody contends.

Lockhart's account, based on presumably accurate information, not merely from his father-in-law's papers, but from Cadell, Constable's partner, is that the losses were due partly to the absolutely unbusinesslike conduct of the concern, and the neglect, for many years, to come to a clear understanding what its profits were and what they were not; partly to the ruinous system of eternally interchanged and renewed bills, so that, for instance, sums which Constable nominally paid years before were not actually liquidated at the time of the smash;

but most of all to a proceeding which seems to pass the bounds of recklessness on one side, and to enter pretty deeply into those of fraud on the other. This is the celebrated affair of the counter-bills, things, according to Lockhart, representing no consideration or value received of any kind, but executed as a sort of collateral security to Constable when he discounted any of John Ballantyne's innumerable acceptances, and intended for use only if the real and original bills were not met. Still, according to Lockhart, this system was continued long after there was any special need for it, and a mass of counter-bills, for which the Ballantynes had never had the slightest value, and the amount of which they had either discharged or stood accountable for already on other documents, was in whole or part flung upon the market by Constable in the months of struggle which preceded his fall, and ranked against Ballantyne & Co, that is to say, Scott, when that fall came.

This account, when published in the first edition of Lockhart's *Life*, provoked strong protests from the representatives of the Ballantynes, and a rather acrimonious pamphlet of war followed, in which Lockhart is accused by some not merely of acrimony, but of a supercilious and contemptuous fashion of dealing with his opponents. He made, however, no important retractions later, and it is fair to say that not one of his allegations has ever been disproved by documentary evidence, as certainly ought to have been possible while all the documents were at hand. Nor did the *Memoirs* of Constable, published many years later, supply what was and is missing; nor does Mr Lang, with all his pains, seem to have found anything decisive.

The assertions opposed to Lockhart's are that the 'counter-bill' story is not true, and that the distresses of Ballantyne & Co, and the dangerous extent to which they were involved in complicated bill transactions with Constable, were at least partly due to reckless drawings by the senior partner – Scott – for his land purchases and other private expenses. Between the two it is impossible to decide with absolute certainty. All that can be said is this.

First, considering that the whole original capital of the firm was Scott's, that he had repeatedly saved it from ruin by his own exertions and credit, and that a very large part of the legitimate grist that came to its mill was supplied by his introduction of work to be printed, he was certainly entitled to the lion's share of any profit that was actually earned. Secondly, the neglect to balance accounts, and the reckless fashion of interweaving acceptance with drawing and drawing with acceptance, had, as we know, been repeatedly protested against by him. Thirdly, his private expenditure, very moderate at Castle Street, and not recklessly lavish even at Abbotsford, must have been amply covered by his official and private income *plus* a small part of the always large and latterly immense funds which for nearly twenty years he had earned from his work as a writer. It is impossible to see that, except by his carelessness in neglecting to ascertain from time to time the exact liabilities of the firm, he had added to the original fault of joining it, or had in any other way deserved the blow that fell upon him. No one can believe, certainly no one has ever proved, that his earnings, and his salaries, and the value of his property, if capitalized, would not have covered, and far more than covered, the cost of Abbotsford, land and house, the settlements on his children, and the household expenses of the whole fifteen years and more since he became a housekeeper there. While, as for the printing business itself, it admittedly ought to have made a handsome profit from first to last, and certainly did make a handsome profit as soon as it fell under reasonably business-like management afterwards.

There remains the said 'original fault' of engaging in the business at all, and that can probably never be denied. The very introduction of joint-stock companies, to which, in part, Scott owed his ruin, has made a confusion between professional and commercial occupations which did not then exist; it would hardly have been considered decent for a public servant, discharging judicial functions, to carry on actual business in a private trading concern. Moreover, the secrecy which

Scott observed – to such an extent that his family and his most intimate friends did not know the facts – could come from nothing but a sense that something was wrong, and certainly led to the commission of much that was so. Scott had to conceal the actual and very material truth when he applied to the Duke of Buccleuch for the guarantee that saved him a dozen years earlier. He had to conceal it from the various persons who employed Ballantyne & Co, and were induced to do so by him. He had to conceal it when he executed those settlements on his son's marriage, which certainly would have been affected had it been known that the whole of his fortune was subject to an unlimited liability.

The mystery of his unconsciousness of all this may be left pretty much where Lockhart, with full acknowledgement, left it. His action seems to have originated partly in a blind and groundless fear of poverty, which, as blind and groundless fear so often does, made him run into the very danger he tried to avoid, partly in a liking for and loyalty towards the Ballantynes that is hard to understand. We have no evidence that can be trusted, that during the entire term of his connection with the firm he derived any positive profit from it that was in any way commensurate with his actual financial investment and the many sacrifices and exertions which he made for the firm's benefit. The whole thing is, once more, a mystery, and the best comment is perhaps the simple one that the means which a man takes to ruin or seriously damage himself generally do seem a mystery to others, and probably are so to himself. Nor is there anything more unusual in the colossal irony of the situation, when we find Scott, just before his own ruin, and in the act of giving his friend Terry the actor a guarantee (which, as it happened, he had to pay), writing words of the most excellent sense on the rashness of engaging in commercial undertakings without sufficient capital, the madness of dealing in bills, and his own resolve to have nothing to do with any business carried on 'by discounts and renewals'. The irony, let it be repeated, is colossal; yet it is equalled and committed every day and everywhere.

It is painful to read that during the months of uncertainty which preceded the actual crash, Scott threw the helve after the hatchet by charging himself personally, first, with an advance, or, at least, a bond for £5,000, and then for another of double that amount, to help two firms, Constable and Hurst & Robinson, whose combined indebtedness was over half a million. But the fact of his doing so was more than enough to indicate the spirit in which he would meet the crash of Ballantyne & Co itself.

The whole of the *Diary* of the period is one long illustration (without the slightest pretentiousness or self-consciousness) of the famous line of perhaps his own greatest poetical passage:

'No thought was there of dastard flight.'

He had made up his mind, before it was certainly imminent, that bankruptcy was not to be accepted; evasion of any more thorough kind, if it occurred, he dismissed at once as not even to be thought of. Yet it is perhaps to be regretted that the mode in which the disaster was actually met, heroic as it was, was chosen in place of that of which he had at first thought – the simple throwing up of every scrap of his property, including all but a bare subsistence out of his official incomes, which could not have been touched without difficulty.

Had he done, or been able to do this, had he shaken off the vampire in stone and lime and hungry soil which had so long sucked his blood, had he sold the library, and the 'Gabions of Jonathan Oldbuck' as he called his collected curios, and the Japanese papers, and the Byron vase, and the armour, had he mortgaged his incomes by help of insurance, sold his copyrights outright, and, in short, realized everything, it is quite possible that he might have been able to raise sufficient funds to pay off his creditors in full, or, at least, to be left with only a small balance which could be discharged by less superhuman and fatal exertions than those actually made. The time was not a good time for selling, no doubt; but, on the other hand, the interest in Abbotsford and its master was still at its height, and the enthusiasm, which actually inspired one anonymous offer of thirty thousand pounds on loan in a lump, would probably have made good bargains for him on sales. He would then have been a free, or nearly a free man, with his own exertions unhampered, or nearly so. He had already had several warnings that his health was in serious danger; and the history of the next six or seven years seems to show that, if he had been able to heed the warnings and not drive himself so hard or so fast and mercilessly, he might have lived for several years more, restored to a better physical state, if not to wealth.

Unfortunately, if nothing else – family affection and perhaps also family pride did still, it may be feared, supply something else to stand in his way – the unlucky settlement of Abbotsford upon his son Walter. Legally, it is true or at least probable, this settlement might have been upset; but the trustees of Mrs Walter Scott would probably also have felt bound to resist this, and leave to unsettle could only have been obtained on the humiliating and even slightly disgraceful plea that the granter, being practically insolvent at the time, was acting beyond his rights. It seems to have been proposed by the Bank of Scotland, during the negotiations for the arrangement which followed, that this should be done; and the reasons which dictated Scott's refusal would have equally, no doubt, prevented him from doing it in the other case.

Accordingly, it was resolved, as he refused to go into bankruptcy, that his whole property should, under a procedure half legal, half amicable, be vested in trustees for the benefit of his creditors; nothing except the Castle Street house and some minor belongings being actually sold. He, on the other hand, undertook to devote to the liquidation of the balance of his debts all the proceeds of his future work, except a bare maintenance for himself and (on a reduced scale) for Abbotsford. How 'this fatal venture of mistaken chivalry' (to borrow a most applicable phrase of Kingsley's about another matter) was carried out we shall see, but how grossly unfair it was to Scott himself must appear at once.

In return for his sacrifices, he had no real legal protection; any creditor could, as a man named Abud actually did, threaten at any time to force bankruptcy unless he were paid at once and in full. Instead of retaining (as he would have done had the whole of his property been actually surrendered, and had he allowed the debts which came with the law to go with it) complete control of his future earnings and exertions, and making, as he might have made, restitution by instalments as a free gift, he was in such a plight that any creditor was entitled to

132

regard him as a kind of slave, paying debt by service as a matter of course, and deserving neither rest, nor gratitude, nor commendation. It is sometimes tempting to regret that Abud or somebody else was not more relentless – to pray for a Sir Giles Overreach or a Shylock among the creditors. For such a person, by his apparently malevolent but really beneficent grasping, would have in effect liberated the bondsman, who, as it was, was forced to labour at a hopeless task to his dying day, and to hasten the dawning of that dying day in the attempt.

Mention has been made above of a certain *Diary* which is our main authority, and, indeed, makes other authorities merely illustrative for a great part of the few and evil last years of Sir Walter's life. It was begun before the calamities, and just after the return from Ireland, and was christened with the name of 'Gurnal', a touching reference to the early childhood speech of his daughter Sophia. It was suggested – and Lockhart seems to think that it was effective – as a relief from the labour of *Napoleon*, which Scott had found to be a difficult task, even before it became bond-work. It may have been a doubtful prescription, for 'the cud of sweet and bitter fancy' is dangerous food. But it has certainly done *us* good.

When Mr Douglas obtained leave to publish it as a whole, there were, it is said, some people who (misguidedly) dreaded the effect of the publication, thinking that the passages which Lockhart himself had left out might in some way diminish and belittle our respect for Scott. They had no need to trouble themselves. It was already, as published in part in the Life, one of the most pathetically interesting things in biographical literature. This quality was increased by the complete publication, while it also became a new proof that 'good blood cannot lie', that the hero is a hero even in utterances kept secret from the very valet. If, as has happened before and might conceivably happen again, some cataclysm destroyed all Scott's other work, we should still have in this not merely an admirable monument of literature, but the picture of a character not inhumanly flawless, yet almost superhumanly noble; of the good man struggling against adversity, not, indeed, with a sham pretence of stoicism, but with that real fortitude of which stoicism is too often merely a caricature and a simulation. It is impossible not to recur to the *Marmion* passage already quoted as one reads the account of the successive misfortunes, the successive expedients resorted to, the absolute determination never to act the coward.

It is from the *Diary* that we learn that he was only too well aware of the fact urged above, that it would have been better for him if his creditors had appeared less favourably disposed towards him. 'If they drag me into court,' he says, 'instead of going into this scheme of arrangement, they would do themselves a great injury, and *perhaps eventually do me good, though it would give me great pain.*' The *Diary*, illustrated as it is by the excellent selections from Skene's *Reminiscences* and other scattered or unpublished matter which Mr Douglas has appended, exhibits the whole history of this period with a precision that could not otherwise have been hoped for, especially as financial misfortunes were soon, as is so often the case in this world, to be complicated by others. For some two years before the catastrophe Lady Scott had been in weak health; and though the misfortune itself does not seem to have affected her much after the first shock, she grew rapidly worse in the spring of 1826, and, her asthma changing into dropsy, died at Abbotsford during Scott's absence in Edinburgh, when his work began in May. His successive references to her illness, and the final and rightly famous passage on her death, are excellent examples of the spirit which pervades this part of the *Diary*. This spirit is never unmanly, but displays throughout, and occasionally, as we see, to his own consciousness, that strange yet not uncommon phenomenon which is well expressed in a French phrase, *il y a quelque chose de cassé* (something is broken), and which frequently comes upon men after or during the greater misfortunes of life. Neither in his references to this, nor in the references to another blow which threatened to strike at around this time, expected from the ever-de-

CHAPTER VI

*L*AST WORKS AND DAYS

It has been mentioned that when Scott returned from Ireland, and before his misfortunes came upon him, he had already engaged in two considerable works; a new novel, *Woodstock*, and a *Life of Napoleon*, planned upon a very large scale, for which Constable made great preparations, and from which he expected enormous profits. After the catastrophe, it became a question whether Constable's estate could claim the fulfilment of these contracts, or whether the profits of them could be devoted wholly to the liquidation of Scott's, or rather Ballantyne & Co's, own debts. The completion of *Woodstock* was naturally delayed until this point was settled. But from the very moment when Sir Walter had resolved to devote himself to the heroic but apparently hopeless task of paying off his nominal liabilities in full, he arranged a system of work upon these two books, and especially upon the *Napoleon*, which, for the dogged determination that it displayed, exceeded anything that even he had done up to this point. The novel was, of course, to him comparative child's play: he had written novels before in six weeks or thereabouts all told, though his impaired strength and energy, the depression of his spirits, and the sense of labouring for the mere purpose of pouring the results into a sieve, made things harder now. But the *Napoleon*, though he had made some preparation for this kind of writing by his elaborate and wide-ranging editorial work, especially by that on Dryden and Swift, was to a great extent new; and it required, to his great irritation, detailed and lengthy research in a large number of books and documents that were relevant to the subject. No man has ever made better use of the results of previous reading for his own pleasure than Scott, and few men, not mere professed book-worms, have ever had vaster stores of it. But he frequently confesses – a confession which in many ways makes his plight in these years all the more tragic – an innate dislike of task-work of any kind; and there is no more laborious task-work than getting up and piecing together the materials for history.

The book, one, at a rough guess, of at least a million words, was completed from end to end in less than eighteen months, during which he also wrote *Woodstock*, *Malachi Malagrowther*, in addition to several reviews and minor pieces. He was also still serving his usual number of days at the Clerk's table, devoting necessarily much time to the painful and equally troublesome business of his financial affairs, his removal from Castle Street, etc., and taking one journey of some length in the summer of 1826 to London and Paris for materials. The feat was accomplished by a rigid system of allocating so much time to the project and setting targets to be achieved every day – a method by which, no doubt, an amount of work, surprising to the inexperienced, can be turned out with no necessarily disastrous consequences. But Scott, disgusted with society, and avoiding it for reasons of economy as well as of want of heart, disturbed hardly at all by strangers at Abbotsford, and not at all in the lodgings and furnished houses which he took while in Edinburgh, let 'his own thought drive him like a goad' to work in the interest of his task-masters, and perhaps, also, for the sake of forcing his own misery to the back of his mind, pushed the system to the most extravagant lengths. It is known that he sometimes worked from six in the morning to six in the evening, with breakfast and lunch brought into his study and eaten there, as he worked. It is probably fortunate that his court duties made this regime impossible for a part of the year, at least during a part of the week, but they did not prevent such efforts entirely. In a period of eighteen months, he cleared for his bloodsuckers nearly twenty thousand pounds, eight thousand for *Woodstock* and eleven or twelve for *Napoleon*. The small profits earned from *Malachi* and the reviews seem to have been permitted to go into his own pocket. He was naturally proud of the exploit, but it is reasonable to suppose that the effort precipitated the end for him.

Of the merits of the *Napoleon* (the second edition of which, by the way, carried its profits to eighteen thousand pounds) it is perhaps not necessary to say very much. It is unlikely that many living persons have read it word for word through, but it is quite possible to form a reasonably well-considered opinion of it without having read the whole. It is only unworthy of its author in the sense that one feels that it is not in any way the work that he was born to do. It is nearly as good, save for the technical inferiority of Scott's prose style, as the historical work of Southey, and very much better than the historical work of Campbell and Moore. The information is sufficient, the narrative clear, and the author can, where necessary, rise to very fair eloquence, or at least rhetoric. But it is too long to be read, as one reads Southey's *Nelson*, for its merits as biography, and not technically authoritative enough to be an exhaustive work of reference from the military, diplomatic, and political side. Above all, one cannot read a page without remembering that there were living then in England at least a dozen men who could have done it better. Grote, Thirlwall, Mitford, Arnold, Hallam, Milman, Lingard, Palgrave, Turner, Roscoe, Carlyle, Macaulay, to mention only the most prominent, and mention them at random, were all alive at the time and capable of such an achievement. There were also probably scores of others who could have done it, by their own choice, nearly or quite as well. On the other hand, there was not one single man living, in England or in the world, who was capable of doing Scott's work of choice; the work which Scott, if not as capable as ever, was still capable of doing like no one before and scarcely any one after him.

Take, for instance, *Woodstock* itself. In a very quaint, characteristic, agreeable, and, as criticism, worthless passage of *Wild Wales*, Borrow has stigmatized it as 'trash'. It is a pity that there is not more such trash outside the forty-eight volumes of the *Waverley Novels*, and there is unlikely to be more. The book, of course, has certain obvious critical faults – which are not in the least what made Borrow object to it. Although Scott, and apparently Ballantyne, liked the catastrophe, it has always seemed to me one of his worst examples of 'huddling up'. For it is historically and dramatically impossible that Cromwell should change his mind, or that Pearson and Robbins should wish to thwart severity which, considering the death of Humgudgeon, had a good deal more excuse than Oliver often thought necessary. Nor may the usual, and perhaps a little more than the usual, shortcomings in construction be denied.

But as of old, and to a greater extent than on some occasions of old, the excellences of character, description, dialogue, and incident are so great as to make recompense, over and over again, for defects of the expected kind. If Everard has something of that unlucky quality which the author recognized in Malcolm Graeme when he said, 'I ducked him in the lake to give him something to do; but wet or dry I could make nothing of him', Alice definitely belongs the better class of his heroines; and from her we ascend to personages in whose case there is very little need of apology and proviso. Sir Henry Lee, Wildrake, Cromwell himself, Charles, may not satisfy some, but most readers are quite content with them; and the famous scene where Wildrake is a witness to Oliver's half-confession can be claimed as one of its author's greatest serious efforts. Trusty Tomkins, perhaps, might have been a little better; he is one of the objects of some unfavourable remarks which Reginald Heber makes in his diary on this class of Scott's figures, though the good bishop may have been rather too severe in his criticism. But the pictures of Woodstock Palace and Park have that indescribable and vivid charm which Scott, without using any of the 'realist' minuteness or 'impressionist' contortions of later days, has the faculty of communicating to such things.

Many readers of Scott's works will happily agree that Tullyveolan, Ellangowan, the Bewcastle moor where Bertram rescued Dandie, Clerihugh's, Monkbarns, the home of the Osbaldistones, and the district from

Aberfoyle to Loch Ard, the moors round Drumclog, Torquilstone, and, not to make the list tedious, a hundred other places, including Woodstock itself, are as real to them as if they had walked over every inch of the ground and sat in every room of the houses. In some cases the supposed originals have not been seen or are unknown; in others, the originals are less striking in fact than they are in Scott's fiction. But in any case these pictures are all real, all possessions, all part of the geographical and architectural furniture of the mind. They are like the wood in the 'Dream of Fair Women': one knows the flowers, one knows the leaves, one knows the battlements and the windows, the platters and the wine-cups, the cabinets and the arras. They are, like all the great places of literature, like Arden and Elsinore, like the court before Agamemnon's palace, and that where the damsel said to Sir Launcelot, 'Fair knight, thou art unhappy', our own – our own to 'pass freely through until the end of time.'

It must not be forgotten in this record of his work that Scott wrote 'Bonnie Dundee' in the very middle of his disaster, and that he had not emerged from the first shock of that disaster, when the astonishingly clever *Letters of Malachi Malagrowther* appeared. The reasonableness of their main purpose – a strenuous opposition to the purpose of doing away, in Scotland as in England, with notes of a smaller denomination than five pounds

– is a matter for debate amongst those who are interested. It is possible that suppressed rage at his own misfortunes found vent, and, for him, very healthy vent, doing no harm to any others, in a somewhat too aggressive patriotism, of a kind more particularist than was usual with him. But the fire and force of the writing are so great, the alternations from seriousness to humour, from denunciation to ridicule, so excellently managed, that there are few better specimens of this particular kind of pamphlet. As for 'Bonnie Dundee', there are hardly two opinions about that. As a whole, it may not be quite equal to 'Lochinvar', to which it forms such an excellent pendant, and which it so nearly resembles in rhythm. But the best of it is equal as poetry, and perhaps superior as meaning. And it admirably completes in verse the tribute long before paid by *Old Mortality* in prose, to the 'last and best of Scots', as Dryden called him in the noble epitaph, which likely inspired Scott himself to do what he could to remove the vulgar aspersions on the fame of the hero of Killiecrankie.

Moreover, according to his habit, Scott had barely finished, indeed he had not finished, the *Napoleon* before he had arranged for new work of two different kinds; and he was soon, without a break, actually engaged upon both tasks, one of them among the happiest things he ever undertook, and the other containing, at least, one piece of his most interesting work. These two new works were the *Tales of a Grandfather* and the *Chronicles of the Canongate*. Both supplied him with his tasks, his daily allowance of 'leaves', for the greater part of 1827, and both were finished and the *Chronicles* actually published, before the end of the same year.

There is not much to recommend in the actual stories comprising these *Chronicles*. The chief in point of size, the *Surgeon's Daughter*, deals with Indian scenes, of which Scott had no direct knowledge, and in connection with which there was no interesting literature to inspire him. It will be totally uninteresting to many readers, more so than *Castle Dangerous* itself. *The Two Drovers* and *The Highland Widow* have more merit; but they are little more than anecdotes.

On the other hand, the 'Introduction' to these *Chronicles*, with the history of their supposed compiler, Mr Chrystal Croftangry, is a thing which can quite reasonably be put on a level with Scott's very greatest work. Much is admittedly personal reminiscence of himself and his friends, handled not with the clumsy and tactless directness of reporting, which has ruined so many novels, but in the great transforming way of Fielding and Thackeray. Chrystal's early thoughtless life, the sketch of his ancestry (said to represent the Scotts of Raeburn), the agony of Mr Somerville, suggested partly by the last illness of Scott's father, the sketches of Janet McEvoy and Mrs Bethune Baliol (Mrs Murray Keith of

Ravelston), the visit to the lost home – all these things are treated not merely with consummate literary effect, but with a sort of muted accompaniment of heart-throbs which only the dullest ear can miss. Nor, as we see from the *Diary*, were the author's recent misfortunes, and his sojourn in a moral counterpart of the Deserted Garden of his friend Campbell, the only disposing causes of this. He had in several ways revived the memory of his early love, Lady Forbes, long since dead. Her husband had been among the most active of his business friends in arranging the compromise with creditors, and was shortly (though Scott did not know it) to discharge privately the claim of the recalcitrant bill-broker Abud, who threatened Sir Walter's personal liberty. Her mother, Lady Jane Stuart, had renewed acquaintance with him, and very soon after the actual publication of the *Chronicles* sent him some manuscript memorials of the days that were long enough ago – memorials causing one of those paroxysms of memory which are the best of all things for a fairly healthy and happy man, but dangerous for one whom time and ill-luck have shaken. He had, while the *Chronicles* were actually in the process of being written, revisited St Andrews, and, while his companions were climbing St Rule's Tower, had sat on a tombstone and remembered how he carved her name in Runic letters thirty-four years before. In short, all the elements, sentimental and circumstantial, of the moment of literary projection were present, and the Introduction was no vulgar piece of 'chemic gold'.

The delightful and universally known *Tales of a Grandfather* present no such contrasts of literary merit, and were connected with no such powerful but exhausting emotions of the mind. They originated in actual stories told to 'Hugh Littlejohn', his grandson, they were encouraged by the fact that there was no popular and readable compendium of Scottish history, they came as easily from his pen as the *Napoleon* had run with difficulty, and are as far removed from hack-work as that vast and, to his creditors, profitable compilation must be pronounced to be on the whole near to it. The book, of course, is not in the modern sense strictly critical, though it must be remembered that the authorities for at least the earlier history of Scotland are so exceedingly few and meagre, that criticism of the saner kind has very little to fasten upon. But in this book eminently, and in the somewhat later compilation for *Lardner's Cyclopaedia* to a rather less degree, this absence of technical criticism is more than made up by Scott's knowledge of humanity, by the divining power, so to say, which his combined affection for the subject and general literary skill gave him, and by that singularly shrewd and pervading common sense, which in him was so miraculously united with the poetical and romantic gift. It is pleasing, but not at all surprising, to note that a professed historian of the time, and one of the best contemporary authorities on the particular subject, when asked what he thought of the general historic effect of Scott's work, answered without the slightest hesitation that it was about the soundest thing, putting mere details aside, that existed on the matter.

It may be observed, in passing, that the later compilation referred to was a marked example of the way in which Scott could at this time 'coin money'. He was offered a thousand pounds for one of the Lardner volumes; and as his sketch swelled beyond the limit, he received fifteen hundred. The entire work, much of which was simple paraphrase of the *Tales*, occupied him, as far as we know, for about six working weeks, or not quite so much. Can it be wondered that both before and after the crash this power of coining money should have put him slightly out of focus with financial matters generally? Mediaeval and other theorizers on usury have been laughed at for their arguments as to the 'unnatural' nature of usurious gain, and its consequent evil. It does not take a particularly superstitious mind to detect a certain unnaturalness in the gift of turning paper into gold in this other way also. Every *peau de chagrin* has a faculty of revenging itself on the possessor.

For the time, however, matters went with Scott as swimmingly as they could with a man who, by his own act, was, as he said, 'eating with spoons and reading books that were not his own', and yet earning by means absolutely within his control, and at his pleasure to exercise or not, some twenty thousand a year. *The Fair Maid of Perth*, a title which has prevailed over what was its first, *St Valentine's Eve*, and has entirely obscured the fact that it was issued as a second series of the *Chronicles of the Canongate*, provided money for a new scheme. This scheme, outlined by Constable himself, and now carried out by Cadell and accepted by Scott's trustees, was for buying in the outstanding copyrights belonging to the bankrupt firm, and issuing the entire series of novels, with new introductions and notes by Scott himself, with attractive illustrations and in a cheap and handy form. Scott himself usually designates the plan as the *Magnum Opus*, or more shortly (and perhaps in rueful memory of more convivial days) 'the *Magnum*'.

The Fair Maid itself was very well received, and seems to have kept its popularity as well as any of the later books. Indeed, the figures of the Smith, of Oliver Proudfute (the last of Scott's humorous-pathetic characters), of the luckless Rothsay, and of Ramornie (who very powerfully affected a generation steeped in Byronism), are all quite up to the author's 'best seconds'. The opening and the close are quite excellent, especially the fight on the North Inch and 'Another for Hector!' and the middle part is full of attractive bits of the kind that contributed to the popularity of older

149

books. But Conachar-Eachin is rather a thing of shreds and patches, and the entire episode of Father Clement and the heresy business is dragged in with singularly little initial excuse, valid connection, or final result.

Unfortunately, there is no diary for the last half of 1828, after Scott returned from a long stay with the Lockharts in London, and as a result little is known of the beginnings of the next novel, *Anne of Geierstein*. When *the Journal* begins again, complaints are heard from Ballantyne. Alterations (which Scott always loathed, and which certainly are detestable things) became or were thought necessary, and when the poor *Maid of the Mist* at last appeared in May 1829, she was dismissed by her begetter very unkindly, as 'not a good girl like the other Annes' – his daughter and her cousin, daughter of Thomas, who were living with him. The book was reasonably well received, but Lockhart is apologetic about it, and it has been the habit of criticism since to share the opinions of 'Aldiborontiphoscophormio', as Scott called James Ballantyne. Nonetheless, many others place *Anne of Geierstein* – as a mere romance and not counting the personal touches which exalt *Redgauntlet* and the Introduction to the *Chronicles* – on a level with anything, and above most things, later than *The Pirate*. Its chief real fault is not so much bad construction – it is actually more, not less, well knit than *The Fair Maid of Perth* – as the too great predominance of merely episodic and unnecessary things and persons, like the *Vehmgericht* and King's Rene's court. Its merits are manifold. The opening storm and Arthur's rescue by Anne, as well as the quarrel with Rudolf, are excellent; the journey (though too much delayed by the said Rudolf's tattlings), with the sojourn at Grafslust and the adventures at La Ferette, ranks with Scott's many admirable journeys, and high among them; Queen Margaret is nobly presented (Shakespeare, Lancastrian that he was, might have enjoyed versifying the scene where she flings the feather and the rose to the winds, as a pendant to 'I called thee then vain shadow of my fortune'); and not only Philipson's rattling peal of thunder to wake Charles the Bold from his stupor, but the Duke's final scenes, come well up to the occasion. Earlier, Scott would not have made Rene quite such a mere old fool, and could have taken the slight touch of pasteboard and sawdust out of the Black Priest of St Paul's. But these are small matters, and the whole merits of the book are not small. Even Arthur and Anne are above, not below, the usual hero and heroine.

The gap in the *Journal* for the last half of 1828 is matched by another and more serious one lasting nearly a year, from July 1829 to May 1830. This was a period during which Sir Walter's health went from bad to worse, and in which he lost his Abbotsford factotum, Tom Purdie. But the first six months of 1829, and perhaps a little more, are among its pleasantest parts.

The shock of the failure and of his wife's death were, as far as might be, over; he had got back into the habit of seeing a fair amount of society; his work, though still busily pursued, was less killing than during the composition of the *Napoleon*; and his affairs were taking a turn for the better. A first distribution, of thirty-two thousand pounds at once, had been made among the creditors. Cadell's scheme of the *Magnum* – wisely agreed to by the trustees, and made possible by a bold purchase at auction of Constable's copyrights for some eight thousand pounds, and later, of those of the poems from Longmans for about the same or a little less – was turning out a great success. They had counted on a sale of eight thousand copies; they had to begin with twelve thousand, and increase it to twenty, while the number ultimately averaged thirty-five thousand. The work of annotation and introduction was not hard, and was decidedly interesting.

Unluckily, irreparable damage to Scott's health had already been done, and when the *Diary* begins again, we soon see signs of it. The actual beginning of the end had occurred before the journal was taken up again, on February 15, 1830. On this day Sir Walter had, in the presence of his daughter and of Miss Violet Lockhart, experienced an attack of an apoplectic-paralytic character, from which he only recovered after much blood-letting and starvation had been prescribed. There can be little doubt that this helped him to make up his mind to do what he had for some time been considering, and resign his place at the Clerk's table: in fact, he probably could not do otherwise. But the results were partly unfortunate. The work had been very easy for him, and had saved him from continual drudgery indoors at home. At the same time, it gave him some company and a change of scene. He was now to live at Abbotsford – for he had neither the means nor the strength to manage a house in Edinburgh that he no longer needed – with surroundings only too likely to encourage 'thick-coming fancies', out of reach of immediate skilled medical attendance, and with very dangerous temptations to carry on over-taxing brain in a manner that was almost deadly to his weakened constitution. Yet he would never give in. The pleasant and not exhausting task of arranging the *Magnum* (which was now bringing in from eight to ten thousand a year for the discharge of his debts) was supplemented by other things, especially *Count Robert of Paris*, and a book on Demonology for Murray's *Family Library*.

He was working on the book on Demonology about the time of his seizure, and after the *Diary* was resumed, it was published in the summer of 1830. Scott was himself by this time conscious of a sort of aphasia of the pen (a direct result of the problem with his brain that had now been diagnosed), and this prevented him sometimes from saying exactly what he wished in a connected manner. The results of this difficulty are in part evident in the book. But it must always remain a blot, quite unforgivable and nearly inexplicable, on the memory of Wilson, that 'Christopher North' allowed himself to comment on some lapses in logic and style in the rude and unkindly way that he did. It is true that he and Scott were at no time very intimate friends, and that there were even some vague antipathies between them. But Wilson owed a considerable debt to Scott in the matter of his professorship; he at least ought to have been nearly as well aware as any of the condition of his benefactor's health; and even if he had known nothing of this, the rest of Sir Walter's circumstances were known to all the world, and should surely have silenced him. But it seems that Wilson was for the moment in dispute with Lockhart, to whom the *Letters on Demonology* were addressed, and so he showed, as he seldom, but sometimes did, the 'black drop', which in his case, though not in Lockhart's, marred at times a generally healthy and noble nature. As a matter of fact, it needs either distinct malevolence or silly hypercriticism to find any serious fault with the *Demonology*. It may not be a masterpiece of scientific treatment in reference to a subject which hardly admits of any such thing. It is, nevertheless, an exceedingly pleasant and amusing and quite uninstructive mixture of learning, traditional anecdote, reminiscence, and story-telling, on a matter which, as is commonly known, had interested the writer from very early days, and which he considered from his usual and invaluable combined standpoint of shrewd sense and poetical appreciation.

His decline, now inevitable and relentless, though its progress was comparatively slow, was more evident in the last two works of fiction which Scott completed, *Count Robert of Parts* and *Castle Dangerous*. Ballantyne and Cadell formally protested against the first ending (no longer in existence) of *Count Robert of Parts*, and Scott rewrote a great deal of it by dictation to Laidlaw. The loss of command both of character and of story-interest is indeed very noticeable. But the opening incident at the Golden Gate, the interview of the Varangian with the Imperial family, the intrusion of Count Robert, and, above all, his battle with the tiger and liberation from the dungeon of the Blachernal, with some other things, show that astonishing power of handling single incidents which was Scott's inseparable gift, and which seems to have remained with him throughout his career to the very eve of his death. The much briefer *Castle Dangerous* (which is connected with an affecting visit of Scott and Lockhart to the tombs of the Douglases) is too slight to give room for very much shortcoming. Its chief artistic fault is the happy ending – for though a romancer is in no way bound to follow his text exactly, and happy endings are quite good things, it is still rather

155

too much to turn upside down the historic catastrophe of the Good Lord James's style of warfare. Otherwise the book is more noticeable for a deficiency of spirit, life, and light – for the evidence of shadow and stagnation falling over the once restless and brilliant scene – than for anything positively bad.

As the author's paralysis prevented him from using his own pen to any great extent, these two books were mainly dictated to William Laidlaw, between the summer of 1830 and the early autumn of 1831. Scott's increasing weakness, and the demands of the *Magnum*, prevented progress from continuing with more speed. The last pages of *Castle Dangerous* contain Scott's farewell, and the announcement to the public of that voyage to Italy which had actually begun when the novels appeared in the month of November.

The period between the fatal seizure and the voyage to the Mediterranean has not much diary concerning it, but has been related with inimitable judgment and sympathy by Lockhart. It was, even putting failing health and obscured mental powers aside, not free from 'browner shades'; for the Reform agitation naturally grieved Sir Walter deeply, while on two occasions he was the object of popular insult and on one of popular violence. Both incidents took place at Jedburgh; but the blame is put upon intrusive weavers from Hawick. The first incident, at a meeting of Roxburghshire freeholders, was nothing more than a rude interruption of a speech made by the author. The speech was almost unintelligible in parts, due to Scott's increasing difficulties in articulation. He felt the criticism bitterly, and when hissing was repeated as he bowed farewell, is said to have replied, low, but now quite distinctly, '*Moriturus vos saluto!*' (I who am about to die, salute you!). On the second occasion, the election after the throwing out of the first Bill, he was stoned, spat upon, and greeted with cries of 'Burke Sir Walter.' Natural indignation has often been expressed at this behaviour towards the best neighbour and the greatest man in Scotland – behaviour which, it is known, haunted him on his deathbed; but it is to be presumed that the people who proclaimed their cause in this way had chosen to conduct themselves in a manner suited to it.

There is no clear evidence to say who it was that first suggested the Italian journey. It could not have been expected to produce any radical cure; but it seems to have been hoped that a change of scene would prevent the patient from succumbing to the temptation to try to write. At Abbotsford it was impossible to keep him from trying, though the effort was simply slow, and not so very slow, suicide. The wishes of his family were most kindly and generously met by the Government of the day, among whose members he had many personal friends, though political opponents; and the frigate *Barham*, a cut-down seventy-four, which had the credit

157

of being one of the smartest vessels in the navy, was assigned to take him to Malta. He had, before he left Abbotsford itself, a moving meeting with Wordsworth, which inspired the writing of *Yarrow Revisited* and the beautiful sonnet, 'A trouble, not of clouds or weeping rain', and had no doubt part in the initiation of the last really great thing that Wordsworth ever wrote – the *Effusion* on the deaths of Hogg, Coleridge, Crabbe, Lamb, and Scott himself, in 1835. The journey was broken for a short while with the Lockharts in London, and again at Portsmouth, waiting for a wind; but the final departure took place on October 29, 1831.

Scott was abroad for the best part of a year, the time being chiefly spent in visits of some length to Malta, Naples, and Rome. There is a good deal of diary for this period, and it, even more than the subsidiary documents and Lockhart's summary of the large amount of writing that is unpublished, betrays the state of the case. Every now and then – indeed, for long passages – there is nothing very different from the state of affairs to which, since the first warning in 1818, the reader has been accustomed. Scott is, if not the infinitely various but never changing Scott of the earlier years, still constant in fun and kindness, in quaint erudition and hearty friendship, though he is all this in a slightly deadened and sicklied degree. But there are strange break-downs and unfamiliar touches. At times he betrays feelings of almost querulous self-concern (something which he had never shown before, in spite of all his difficulties), as where he complains that his companions, his son and daughter, 'are neither desirous to follow his amusements nor anxious that he should adopt theirs'. At other times he shows a certain callousness – still more strange to his nature – as where he dismisses the news of the death of Hugh Littlejohn, whose illnesses earlier had been almost his greatest concern, and records in the same entry that he 'went to the opera.'

The passage in the Introduction to the *Chronicles*, written not so very long before, traces with an almost horrible exactness the changes which were now taking place in himself. Moreover, he insisted on picking up his pen once again; and, first in Malta, then in Naples, began and went far to complete two new novels, *The Siege of Malta* and *Il Bizarro*. These were unpublished at the time of his death and Lockhart resisted attempts to publish them posthumously. Scott had now (it does not seem clear on what grounds, or by what stages) become absolutely convinced that he had paid off all his debts, instead of nearly half of them. Accordingly, he worked out various schemes on which to spend the profits of these works, added to the (as he thought) liberated returns of the *Magnum*; and even revived his old dreams of buying Faldonside with its thousand acres, and 'holding all Tweedbank, from Ettrick-foot to Calla weel.' Feted, too, as he was, and in this condition of mind, it seems to have been difficult for his companions to make him observe the absolute temperance in food and drink which was as necessary to the staving off of the end as abstinence from mental strain. The fact that Scott's beleaguered constitution held out as long as it did under such poor treatment must stand as a testament to its extraordinary strength.

At last, and of course suddenly, came the final warning of all: the occurrence, without notice, of an almost agonising home-sickness. The party travelled by land, as speedily as they could, to the Channel, but a last attack of apoplectic paralysis took hold of Scott at Nimeguen. After crossing the Channel and reaching London, Sir Walter was taken by sea to the Forth, and from there to his home. Death was delayed for only a short time, and the account of his death has been given by Lockhart in one of those great passages of English literature on which it is folly to attempt to improve or even to comment, and which, a hundred times quoted, can never be stale. Sir Walter Scott died at Abbotsford on September 21, 1832, and was buried four days later at Dryburgh. A post-mortem examination had disclosed considerable softening of the brain.

There remained unpaid at his death about fifty-five thousand pounds of the Ballantyne debts, besides private encumbrances on Abbotsford, etc., including the ten thousand which Constable had extracted, he knowing, from Scott unknowing, the extent of the ruin, in the hours just before it. The cashing in of assurances cleared off two fifths of this balance, and Cadell discharged the rest on the security of the *Magnum*, which was equal, though not much more than equal, to the burden in the longrun. Thus, if Scott's exertions during the last seven years of his life had benefited his own pocket instead of those of his creditors, his ambition – whether wise or foolish, the reader must decide – would have been amply fulfilled, and his son, supposing the money to have been invested with ordinary care and luck, would have been left a baronet and squire, with at least six or seven thousand a year. As it was, he did not succeed to much more than the title, a costly house, and a not very profitable estate, burdened, though not heavily, with mortgages. This burden was reduced by the good sense of the managers of the English memorial subscription to Scott, who devoted the six or seven thousand pounds, remaining after some embezzlement, to clearing off the remaining commitment as far as possible. The many financial tributes from Scottish sources funded the erection of the well-known Scott Monument on the edge of Princes Street Gardens in Edinburgh, arguably one of the very few successful things of the kind in the British Isles. Some years later, another monument was set up to the author in Westminster Abbey.

161

CHAPTER

VII

CONCLUSION

It is only natural, and perhaps may be taken as a sign of the great respect that is felt for Scott, both as a gentleman and as a writer, that the tragic close of such a brilliant a career as his should attract rather disproportionate attention. Accordingly, readers of his life show a marked tendency either to feel pity for his calamities, or express admiration for his courage and determination to battle against the greatest of odds, or to engage in moral debate on the 'dram of eale' that was his own share in causing his misfortunes. Undoubtedly, all of these things ought to be considered. But, in the strict court of literary and critical audit, they must not have more than their share. As a matter of fact, Scott's work was almost finished – nothing distinctly novel in kind and first-rate in quality, except the *Tales of a Grandfather* and the Introduction to the *Chronicles*, remained to be added to it – when the terrible financial crisis struck. And the trials which followed, though they showed the strength, the nobleness, the rare balance and solidity of his character, did not create these virtues; they had been formed and established by habit long before. *Respice finem* is not here a wise, at least a sufficient, maxim: we must take a look at his life and work as a continuous whole in order to find out exactly what kind of man Scott was in conduct and in letters.

What kind of man he was physically is pretty well-known from the great number of original portraits in existence, as well as the vast number of reproductions of varying quality. He was not very tall, but of a reasonable height, although his lameness and broad build made him look shorter than he was. His head was distinguished by a peculiar domed, or coned, cranium. This made 'Lord Peter' Robertson give him the nickname of 'Peveril of the Peak', a title which he himself later adopted, and which, shortened to 'Peveril', was commonly used by his family. His expression, according to information from those who saw him and the mood in which he found himself, has been variously described as 'heavy', 'homely', and in similar, but more complimentary terms. But those who knew and appreciated him recognized the curiously combined humour, shrewdness, and kindliness which animated features that were naturally irregular and quite devoid of what his own generation would have called 'chiselled elegance'. He himself maintained – and it seems to be the fact – that from the time of his recovery from his childhood illness to the attack of cramp, or gallstones, or whatever the problem was which came on in 1818, and from which he never really recovered, his health was particularly good; and as a young man he is known to have put it to considerable tests with his fondness for alcohol and an active social life, combined with his love of sport and walking.

His conversation, like his countenance, has been variously characterized. It is most likely that the complexion of both depended, even more than it does with most men, on his company. It is said that he was never boastful or unreasonably argumentative in conversation. He had a very strong dislike of talking about his own work, and although he was happy to talk about literature in general, he was never bookish. He is remembered as a great tale-teller, but was never criticized for monopolizing the conversation in any way. By his own admission, he quite enjoyed periods of solitude in his youth and early middle age. But although he was never truly gregarious, he mixed, from an early age, with people from all walks of life and all levels of society, a fact of which he was justifiably proud. The perfect ease of his correspondence with all sorts and conditions of men and women may have owed something to this; but, no doubt, it owed as much to his own naturally agreeable nature and genuine and intelligent interest in humanity.

The only fault or faults of which he has been accused with any plausibility are those which relate to his attitude to money and the trappings of wealth – that is to say, it was claimed that he was too eager to obtain these things, and at the same time he showed too great a deference for those who possessed them. He cannot be said to have been greedy in the strict sense of the word. He was extraordinarily generous, but not ostentatious. His generosity was almost indiscriminate – some would say foolish. He certainly took no pleasure in hoarding money, and his personal tastes, with the exception of books, and the curios he loved, were hardly extravagant.

But still he was never quite content with an income which, after very early years, was always more than sufficient, and when he launched into commercial ventures, quite considerable, at first in prospect and then in fact. At the same time, he did spend to excess on his house at Abbotsford and surrounding lands and he seems to have been really indifferent about his title, except as an adjunct to these possessions, and as something which could be handed on to, and distinguish, the family he longed to found. Yet no instance of the slightest servility on his part to rank – much less to riches – has been produced. His address, no doubt, both in writing and conversation, was more ceremonious than would now be customary. But it must be remembered that this was then a point of good manners, and that 'your Lordship' and 'my noble friend', even between persons who knew

165

each other very well and shared the same rank in society, were then phrases considered quite proper and usual in private as well as in public life. Attempts have been made to excuse his attitude, on the plea that it was inherited from his father, that it was national, that it was this, that, and the other. But it was no more than the due application to etiquette of the rule of distributive justice, to give every man his own. Scott would probably have accepted the principle, though not the application, of the sentence of Timoleon de Cosse, Duke of Brissac – 'God has made thee a gentleman, and the king has made thee a duke'. And he honoured God and the king by behaving accordingly.

There is a great amount of evidence to show that Scott was a generous host, a charming guest, and a kind and loyal friend and relation. It does not appear that he ever lost an old friend; and though, like most men who have more talent for friendship than for acquaintance, he did not in later life make many new ones, the relations existing between himself and Lockhart are sufficient proof of his ability to play the most difficult of all parts, that of elder friend to younger. He was not one to take offence without good reason, but he was a very dangerous person to take a liberty with; he adopted to the full the morality of his time about duelling, though he disapproved of it; he was in all respects a man of the world, yet without guile.

166

It is quite certain that Scott, though he never talked much about religion (as, indeed, he never talked much about any of the deeper feelings of the heart), was a sincerely religious man. He was not a metaphysician in any way, and therefore had no special inclination towards the serious study of theology, or to theological debate. It is also clear that he did not argue or agonize over specific points of religious doctrine. But there is no doubt whatever that he was a thoroughly and sincerely orthodox Christian. He did his best to live according to his beliefs; and if he did not keep himself (in the matter of the secret partnership and others) altogether unspotted by the sins the world, the sufferings of his last seven years may surely be taken as more than sufficient purification.

Few men have been more blameless morally; fewer still better equipped with the positive virtues. And, above all, there can be seen in Scott a quality that has been already called a certain nobleness, a certain natural inclination towards all things high, and great, and pure, and of good report, which is rarer still than negative blamelessness or even than positive virtue.

To speak of Scott's politics is a little difficult and perhaps a little dangerous; yet they played so large a part in his life and work that the subject can hardly be omitted, especially as it comes just between those aspects of him which we have already discussed, and those to which we are coming. It has sometimes been disputed whether his Toryism was much more than mere sentiment; and of course there were plenty of people in his own day willing to stoop so low as to represent it as mere self-interest. But few people nowadays would doubt, however critical they are of Scott's political creed, that that creed was part, not of his interests, not even of his mere fads and fancies, literary and other, but of his inmost heart and soul. That reverence for the past, that distaste for the vulgar, that sense of continuity, of mystery, of something beyond interest and calculation, which even the enemies of Toryism would possibly admit to be its nobler elements, were the blood of Scott's veins, the breath of his nostrils, the marrow of his bones.

But greater consideration should be shown here to his mental character than to his moral. We must consider him rather as a man of genius than as a man of good, though it is impossible to overlook, and difficult to overestimate, his particular importance as both combined. A reasonably detailed view of his actual literary accomplishment has already been given in this book, and an estimate of the value of each sphere of accomplishment has been attempted. They must be considered as a whole in order to answer the following questions – first, What were the peculiar characteristics of his thought? and, secondly, What distinguished his expression of this thought?

With regard to the characterisitics of his thought, it is generally admitted that he did not indulge in intellectual analysis or detailed argument about character, or morality. But to proceed from this admission to a general denial of 'philosophy' to him – that is to say, to allow him a merely superficial knowledge of human nature – is a complete mistake. There is more philosophy in his writing than there is in some of the great philosophical works. This statement might be supported with a large anthology of passages in the novels and even the poems – passages indicating an anthropological science as intimate as it is unpretentiously expressed.

To some good folk in our days, who think that nothing can be profound which is naturally and simply spoken, and who demand that a human philosopher shall speak gibberish and wear his boots on his brows, the fact may be strange, but it is a fact. And it may be added that even if chapter and verse could not thus be produced, a sufficient proof, the most sufficient possible, could be otherwise provided.

Scott, as all competent judges of literature save a very few will admit, has created almost more men and women, undoubtedly real and lifelike, than any other prose novelist. Now you cannot create a man or a woman without knowing whereof a man and a woman are made. Scott was happy to put his great knowledge of human-

169

ity, his science, into practice rather than to expound it in theory. He preferred to demonstrate it rather than to lecture on it.

Nor did Scott demonstrate any intensity of personal passion in his writing, especially in the sense to which that word is more commonly confined. He has nowhere left us (as some other men of letters have) any hint that he refrained from doing this because the passion would have been so tremendous that it was on the whole best for mankind that they should not be exposed to it. The qualities of humour and of taste which were always present with Scott would have prevented this. It is doubtful whether he felt any temptation to open his heart, or any need to do so. The slight hints given at the time of the combined action of his misfortunes and the agitation arising from his renewed communications with Lady Jane Stuart, are almost all the indications that we have on the subject, and they are too slight to found any theory upon. It is clear that this was not his vein, or that, if the vein was there, he did not choose to work it.

The region in which Scott's power of conception and expression did lie, and which he ruled with wondrous range and rarely equalled power, was a strangely united kingdom of common-sense fact and fanciful or traditional romance. No writer who has had such a sense of the past, of tradition, of romantic literature, has had such a grasp of the actual working motives and conduct of mankind; none who has had the latter has even come near to Scott's command of the former. We may take Spenser and Fielding as the princes of these separate principalities in English literature, and though each had gifts that Scott had not – though Scott had gifts possessed by neither – yet if a blend of Spenser and Fielding could be imagined, the blend would, possibly, come nearer to Scott's idiosyncrasy than anything else that can be imagined.

He had advanced (or rather turned away) from that one-sided eighteenth-century conception of nature which was content to know *human* nature pretty thoroughly up to a certain point, and to dismiss 'prospects' (natural scenes), in Johnson's scornful language to Thrale, as one just like the other. But he had kept the eighteenth century grasp of man himself, while recovering the path to wonderful places such as the Idle Lake and the Cave of Despair, to the many treed wood through which Una and her knight journeyed, and the Rich Strand where all the treasures of antiquity lay. This was an achievement unequalled in his time, and for some time to come.

Scott's other special literary characteristic, next to that really magical faculty, which has already been mentioned, of placing scenes and peopling them with characters in the memory of his readers, is his humour. It is a good

171

old scholastic doctrine, that the greatest merit of anything is to be excellent in the special excellence of its
kind. And in that quality which so gloriously differenti-
ates English literature from all others, Scott is never
wanting, and is almost always pre-eminent. If his patriotism, intense as it is, is never grotesque or offensive, as
patriotism too often is to readers who do not share it; if
his pathos never touches the maudlin; if his romantic
sentiment is always saved by the sense of solid fact – and
we may assert these things without hesitation or quali-
fication – it is due to his humour.

For this humour, never merely local, never bases its
appeal on small private sympathies and understandings
and passwords which leave the world at large cold, or
mystified, or even disgusted. He has used rather than
abused dialect to add to the appeal of this humour, in a
manner skilful enough to attract the admiration of almost all good judges, and too judicious for his followers, defying their attempts to emulate him in this respect. And, further, the universal quality of his humour
is free from some accompanying drawbacks which must
be acknowledged in the humour of some of the other
very great humorists. It is not coarse – a defect which
has made prigs throughout the ages affect horror at
Aristophanes; it is not grim, like that of Swift; it is free
from any very strong evidences of its owner having lived
at a particular date, such as may be detected by the Dev-

il's Advocate even in Fielding, even in Thackeray. No tricks or grimaces, no mere elaboration, no lingering for imagined applause; but a moment of life and nature subjected to the humour-stamp and left recorded and transformed for ever – there is Scott.

That the necessary counterpart and companion of this breadth of humour should be depth of feeling can be no surprise to those who accept the only sound distinction between humour and wit. Scott himself never wore his heart on his sleeve; but to those who looked a little farther than the sleeve its beatings were sufficiently evident. The Scott who made that memorable exclamation on the Mound, and ejaculated 'No, by – !' at the discovery of the Regalia, who wrote Jeanie's speech to Queen Caroline and Habakkuk Mucklewrath's to Claverhouse, had no need ever to affect emotion, because it was always present, though repressed when it had no business to show itself.

His romantic imagination was as sincere as his pathos or his indignation. He never lost the clue to 'the shores of old romance'; and, at least, a great part of the secret which made him such a magician to his readers was that the spell was on himself – that the regions of fancy were as open, as familiar as Princes Street or the Parliament Square to this solid practical Clerk of Session, who claimed that no food could to his taste equal Scotch broth, and who was, in everything but the one fatal delusion, as sound a man of business as ever partook of that nourishing concoction.

In his execution both in prose and verse, but more obviously or particularly in the latter there are certain peculiarities, in the nature (at least partly) of defect, which strike every critical eye at once. At no time, and in no case, was Scott one of these careful, anxious miniaturists of work, who repaint every stroke a hundred times, adjust every detail of composition over and over again, and can never be finished with rehandling and perfecting.

Nor did he belong to that very rare class whose work seems to be faultless from the first, or at any rate after a very short apprenticeship, to whom inelegancies of style, incorrect rhymes, licences of metre – not deliberate and intended to produce the effect they achieve, but the effect of carelessness or of momentary inability to do what is wanted – are by nature or education impossible. He was not blessed with such a nature, and his education was of the very last sort to procure it for him. He himself, not out of pique or conceit, things utterly alien from his nature, still less out of laziness, but as a genuine, and, what is more, a correct self-criticism, has left in his private writings repeated expressions of his belief that revision and correction in his case not only failed to improve the work, but were in most cases likely to do it positive harm, that the spoon was made or the horn spoiled (to adapt his country proverb) at the first draft, and once for all. This was probably a correct judgment, and yet it does not imply any inferiority on his part. It is not as if he ever aimed at the methods of the precisians and failed, as if it was his desire to be a 'correct' writer, a careful observer of proportion and construction, a producer of artful felicities in metre, rhythm, rhyme, phrase.

We may yield to no one in the delight of tracing the exact correspondence of strophe and antistrophe in a Greek chorus, the subtle vowel-music of a Latin hymn or a passage of Rossetti's. But there is no reason, because we rejoice in these things, why we should demand them of all poetry, or why, because we rejoice in the faultless construction of Fielding or the exquisite finish of Jane Austen as novelists, we should despise the looser handling and more sweeping touch of Scott in prose fiction. It is extremely probable that this breadth of touch obtained him his popularity abroad, and it should not impair his fame at home.

Unquestionably, though he had many minor gifts and graces, including that of incomparable lyric snatch, from the drums and fifes of 'Lochinvar' and 'Bonnie Dundee' to the elfin music of 'Proud Maisie', his faculty of weaving a story in prose or in verse, with varied decorations of dialogue and description and character, rather than on a cunning canvas of plot, was Scott's main forte. If it is in verse, although admittedly admirable, less pre-eminent than in prose, it is, first, because minor formal defects are more felt in verse than in prose; secondly, because the scope of the medium is less; and thirdly, because the medium itself was in reality not what he wanted. The verse romance of Scott is a great achievement and a delightful possession: it has had extraordinary influence on English literature, from the work of Byron, which it directly produced, and which pretty certainly would never have been produced without it, to that of Mr William Morris, which may possibly have been its last echo – transformed and refreshed, but still an echo – for some time to come. But there was a little of the falsetto in it, and the interludes, of which the introductions to *Marmion* and to the *Bridal* are the most considerable, show that it gave no outlets, or outlets only awkward, for much of what he wanted to say.

He defines his own general literary object admirably in a letter to Morritt. 'I have tried to induce the public to relax some of the rules of criticism, and to be amused with that medley of tragic and comic with which life presents us, not only in the same course of action, but in the same character.' The detailed remarks which have been given in earlier chapters make it unnecessary to bring out the application of this to all his work, both verse and prose. And it need only be pointed out in passing how much more satisfactorily the form of prose fiction lent itself, than the form of verse romance, to the expression of a creed which, as it had been that of Shakespeare, so it was the creed of Scott.

But a few words must be added in reference to the complaint which is often openly made, and which is still more often secretly entertained, or taken for proved, by the younger generation – to wit, the complaint that Scott is 'commonplace' and 'conventional', not merely in thought, but in expression. As to the thought, that is best met by the reply churlish, if not even by the reproof valiant. Scott's thought is never commonplace, and never merely conventional: it can only seem so to those who have given their own judgments in bondage to a conventional and temporary cant of unconventionality. In respect of expression, the complaint will admit of some argument which may best take the form of example.

It is perfectly true that Scott's expression is not 'quintessenced' – that it has to a hasty eye an air of lacking what is called distinction; and, especially, that it has no very definite savour of any particular time. In most periods during the recorded story of literature, there is a marked preference for all these things which it is not; and so Scott has been, with certain persons, in disfavour accordingly. But it so happens that the study of this now long record of literature is itself sufficient to convince anyone how treacherous the tests thus suggested are. There never, for instance, was an English writer fuller of all the marks which the younger critics of the earlier twentieth century, longed for in Scott, and admired in some authors of their own day, than John Lyly, the author of *Euphues*, of a large handful of very charming and interesting court dramas, and of some delightful lyrics. Those who had to teach literature impressed the importance, and try to impressed the interest, of Lyly on students and readers, and they did right. For he was a man not merely of talent, but also of genius.

He had a poetical fancy, a keen and biting wit, a fairly exact proficiency in the scholarship of his time. He rejected the obvious, the commonplace in thought, and still more in style, as passionately as any man ever had rejected it, and, having not merely will and delicacy, but power, he not only achieved an immense temporary popularity, but even influenced the English language permanently. Yet – and those who thus praised him knew it – he, the apostle of ornate prose, the model of a whole generation of the greatest wits that England has seen, the master of Shakespeare in more things than one, including romantic comedy, the originator of the English analytic novel, the 'raiser' of his native language to a higher power, was already dead.

We shall never get anybody outside the necessarily small number of those who have cultivated the historic as well as the aesthetic sense in literature, to read him except as a curiosity or a task, because he not merely cultivated art, but neglected nature for it; because he fooled the time to the top of its bent, and let the time fool him in return; because, instead of making the common as though it were not common, he aimed and strained at the uncommon *in* and *per se.*

Scott did just the contrary. He never tried to be unlike somebody else; if he hit, as he did hit, upon great new styles of literature – absolutely new in the case of the historical novel, revived after long trance in the case of the verse tale – it was from no desire to innovate, but because his genius called him. Though in ordinary ways he was very much a man of his time, he did not contort himself in any fashion by way of expressing a (then) modern spirit, a Georgian idiosyncrasy, or anything of that sort; he was content with the language of the best writers and the thoughts of the best men. He was no amateur of the topsy-turvy, and had not the very slightest desire to show how a literary head could grow beneath the shoulders. He was satisfied that his genius should flow naturally. And the consequence is that it was never checked, that it flows still for us with all its spontaneous charm, and that it will flow for all time to come.

Among many instances of the strength which accompanied this absence of strain, one already alluded to may be mentioned again. Scott is one of the most literary of all writers. He was saturated with reading; nothing could happen but it brought some felicitous quotation, some quaint parallel to his mind from the great wits, or the small, of old. Yet no writer is less *bookish* than he; none insults his readers less with any parade, with any apparent awareness of his own erudition; and he wears his learning so lightly that pedants have even accused him of lacking it because he lacks pedantry.

His stream, to resume the metaphor, carries in solution more reading as well as more wit, more knowledge of life and nature, more gifts of almost all kinds than would suffice for twenty men of letters, yet the very power of its solvent force, as well as the vigour of its current, makes these things comparatively invisible.

In dealing with an author so voluminous and so various in his kinds and subjects of composition, it is a hard matter to say what has to be said within prescribed limits such as these, just as it is still harder to select from so copious a store of biographical information details which may be sufficient, and not more than sufficient, to give a firm and distinct picture of his life. Yet it may perhaps be questioned whether very elaborate handling is necessary for Scott. No man probably, certainly no man of letters, is more of a piece than he. As he has been subjected to an almost unparalleled trial in the revelation of his private thoughts, so his literary powers and performances extend over a range which is unusual, and absolutely outstanding, in men of letters of the highest rank. Yet he is the same throughout, in romance as in review, in novel as in note-writing.

Except his dramatic work, a department for which he seems to have been almost totally unfitted (despite the felicity of his 'Old Play' fragments), nothing of his can be neglected by those who wish to enjoy him to the full. Yet though there is no monotony, there is a uniformity which is all the more delightfully brought out by the minor variations of subject and kind. The last as the first word about Scott should perhaps be, 'Read him. And, as far as possible, read all of him.'

In comparatively early days of his acquaintance with Lockhart, Scott, suffering from the terrible pains of his cramps and thinking himself near death, bequeathed to his future son-in-law, in the words of the ballad, 'the vanguard of the three', the duty of burying him and continuing his work, if possible. In doing so, he had himself limited the heritage to the defence of ancient faith and loyalty – a great one enough.

But his heritage is, in fact, a greater one than that. From generation to generation, whosoever determines, in so far as fate and the gods allow, to hold these things fast, and, moreover, to love all good literature, to temper learning with common sense, to let humour wait always upon fancy, and duty upon romance; whosoever at least tries to be true to the past, to face the present with courage, and to let the future be as it may; whosoever 'spurns the vulgar' while trying to be fair to all individuals, and faces 'the Secret' with neither bravado nor cringing – he may take, if not the vanguard, yet a place according to his worth and merit, in the legion which this great captain led.

Of the frequent parallels or contrasts drawn between him and Shakespeare it is to be noted that Scott is, of all men of letters, one of whom we have some of the most intimate and the fullest knowledge, while of Shakespeare we have the least. There need be very little doubt that if we knew everything about Shakespeare, he would come, as a man of mould might, scathless from the test. But we do know everything, or almost everything, about Scott, and he comes out nearly as well as anyone but a faultless monster could.

For all the great works of literature, as for other things, let us be thankful – for Blake and for Beddoes as well as for Shelley and for Swift. But let everyone who for himself, or through his ancestors, claims origin between Tol-Pedn-Penwith and Dunnet Head,

be energetic and confident in expressing his gratitude for the fact that his is the race and his the language of Sir Walter Scott.

CHRONOLOGY

1771 Sir Walter Scott, son of Walter Scott, a writer to the Signet, and Anne Rutherford, is born at the top of College Wynd, Edinburgh.

1779 Much of Scott's early youth is spent on his grandfather's farm in the Borders, but in 1779 he returns to Edinburgh where he is educated at Edinburgh High School and University.

1786 Scott is apprenticed to his father at the age of fifteen, as a useful preparation for his career. From his fifteenth year until his marriage, he visits many parts of Scotland.

1792 In July, Scott is called to the Bar.

1794 In April, Scott takes part (victoriously) in a series of battles with sticks, between Loyalist advocates and writers and Irish Jacobin medical students, in the pit of the Edinburgh theatre.

1795 In June, Scott becomes a curator of the Advocates' Library.

1796 In October, Scott's first work, consisting of translations of Bürger's *Lenore* and *Der Wilde Jäger* (*The Wild Huntsman*), is published.

1797 In the spring and summer of 1797, Scott becomes quartermaster, paymaster, secretary and captain in the Edinburgh Light Horse.

In October, Scott becomes engaged to Charlotte Margaret Carpenter, or Charpentier, and they are married on Christmas Eve in Carlisle.

The young couple take up residence in Castle Street which is to be Charlotte's home for the rest of her Edinburgh life.

1798 Scott's first child is born on the 14 October but does not live many hours.

1799 February sees the publication of Scott's second volume, the translation of Goethe's *Götz von Berlichingen*.

In March, Scott and his wife go to London. His father dies during this visit.

Scott inherits some property from his father and legacies from relations add more to his income.

In November, Scott's son Walter is born.

In December, Scott is appointed Sheriff-Depute of Selkirkshire.

1801 In October, Scott's daugher Sophia is born.

1802 The *Edinburgh Review* (to which Scott contributes) is started. Later Scott secedes from it due to its Whig attitude.

The first two volumes of Scott's *Minstrelsy of the Scottish Border* are published.

1803 In February, Scott's daughter Anne is born.

The third volume of Scott's *Minstrelsy of the Scottish Border* appears and *Sir Tristrem* (which is in a way a fourth) is not very long in following.

1805 *The Lay of the Last Minstrel* is published in the first week of January.

Scott enters into partnership with James Ballantyne.

In December, Scott's son, Charles, is born.

1808 *Marmion* is published in February and *Dryden* in April 1808.

1809 Scott promotes the creation of the Tory *Quarterly Review*

1810 *The Lady of the Lake*, the first of Scott's quintet of long poems, is published and at once becomes enormously popular.

Scott resumes the writing of *Waverley*, a complete change in the direction of his literature.

1811 Scott purchases Abbotsford on the Tweed.

1812 Scott's poem *Rokeby* , the second of the long poems, is dated on the very last day of 1812.

1813 *Rokeby* and *The Bridal of Triermain* are published.

Scott refuses the poet laureateship and recommends Southey for the honour.

1814 June sees the completion, in about three weeks, of the last half of *Waverley*. It and the rest of his novels first appear anonymously.

The poem, *The Lord of the Isles*, appears in December.

1815 *Guy Mannering* is published.

1816 *Paul's Letters to his Kinsfolk* is published.
The Antiquary, *Old Mortality* and *The Black Dwarf* are published.

1817 *Harold the Dauntless*, the last of the long poems, is published.
The Regalia of Scotland are rediscovered at Edinburgh Castle, a triumph in which Scott plays a leading role.

1818 In June, *The Heart of Midlothian* is published.
The Duke of Buccleuch, Scott's patron, his helper in time of need, and his most intimate friend, dies.

1819 Scott purchases a commission for his son, Walter, in the Eighteenth Hussars.
The Bride of Lammermoor, *A Legend of Montrose* and *Ivanhoe* are published.

1820 In April, Scott receives his baronetcy.
The Monastery and *The Abbot* are published.

1821 *Kenilworth* and *The Pirate* are published.

1822 *The Fortunes of Nigel* is published.
George IV visits Scotland and Scott plays a major part in all the proceedings.

1823 *Peveril of the Peak*, *St Ronan's Well* and *Quentin Durward* are published.

1824 *Redgauntlet* is the last full-length novel to be published before the downfall of Ballantyne & Co.

1825 The estate of Abbotsford is practically completed and is used to celebrate the marriage in February of Scott's son and heir, Walter.

1826 James Ballantyne & Co. become involved in the bankruptcy of Constable & Company. Scott, as a partner of the former, finds himself liable for a debt of some £117,000. Scott works heroically from now on to pay off the creditors, who receive full payment after his death.

Lady Scott dies at Abbotsford in May.

Woodstock is published.

1827 Scott admits to the authorship of his novels.

1828 *The Fair Maid of Perth* is published.

1829 *Anne of Geierstein* and *The Maid of the Mist* are published.

1830 In February Scott has another stroke.

1831 *Count Robert of Paris* and *Castle Dangerous* are published.

Scott travels abroad for the best part of a year.

1832 While abroad, Scott experiences a bout of severe homesickness and travels home to Abbotsford, where he dies on 21 September.

Scott is buried on 25 September at Dryburgh.